The Early Modern Englishwoman:
A Facsimile Library of Essential Works

Series I

Printed Writings, 1500–1640: Part 3

Volume 2

Judith Man

The Early Modern Englishwoman:
A Facsimile Library of Essential Works

Series I

Printed Writings, 1500–1640: Part 3

Volume 2

Judith Man

Selected and Introduced by
Amelia A. Zurcher

General Editors
Betty S. Travitsky and Anne Lake Prescott

ASHGATE

Published by
Ashgate Publishing Limited
Wey Court East
Union Road
Farnham
Surrey, GU9 7PT
England

Ashgate Publishing Company
110 Cherry Street
Suite 3-1
Burlington
VT 05401-3818
USA

Ashgate website: http://www.ashgate.com

British Library Cataloguing-in-Publication Data
Man, Judith
    Judith Man. – (The early modern Englishwoman : a facsimile
    library of essential works. Printed writings 1500–1640,
    series I, part 3, vol. 2)
    1. Romance fiction   2. French literature – 16th Century
    3. English literature – Early modern, 1500–1700
    I. Title   II. Zurcher, Amelia A.
    843.3

Library of Congress Cataloging-in-Publication Data
The early modern Englishwoman: a facsimile library of essential works. Part 3. Printed Writings 1500–1640 / general editors, Betty S. Travitsky and Anne Lake Prescott.

See page vi for complete CIP Block 2002025878

The woodcut reproduced on the title page and on the case is from the title page of Margaret Roper's trans. of [Desiderius Erasmus] *A Devout Treatise upon the Pater Noster* (circa 1524).

ISBN 978-0-7546-0441-9

Transfered to Digital Printing in 2010

MIX
Paper from
responsible sources
FSC® C004959

Printed and bound in Great Britain
by Printondemand-worldwide.com

CONTENTS

Library of Congress Cataloging-in-Publication Data
Coeffeteau, Nicolas, 1574–1623.
    [Histoire de Poliarque et d'Argenis. English]
    Judith Man / [selected and introduced by] Amelia A. Zurcher.
       p. cm.– (The early modern Englishwoman. Printed writings,
1500–1640, Series 1, Part 3 ; v. 2)
"An epitome of the history of faire Argenis and Polyarchus is Judith
Man's English translation of a 1623 French work by Nicholas Coeffeteau,
Histoire de Poliarque et d'Argenis, which is itself an abridgement and
translation of one of the most widely read fictional works of the
seventeenth cetury, John Barclay's 1621 Latin romance Argenis"--P. 1.
Includes bibliographical references.
    ISBN 0-7546-0441-1 (alk. paper)
    I. Man, Judith. II. Zurcher, Amelia A., 1965-. III. Coeffeteau,
Nicolas, 1574–1623. Epitome of the history of faire Argenis and
Polyarchus. IV. Barclay, John, 1582–1621. Argenis. V. Title. VI. Series.

PQ1737 .C58 H5713 2002
873'.04--dc21

                    2002025878

PREFACE
BY THE GENERAL EDITORS

Until very recently, scholars of the early modern period have assumed that there were no Judith Shakespeares in early modern England. Much of the energy of the current generation of scholars has been devoted to constructing a history of early modern England that takes into account what women actually wrote, what women actually read, and what women actually did. In so doing the masculinist representation of early modern women, both in their own time and ours, is deconstructed. The study of early modern women has thus become one of the most important—indeed perhaps the most important—means for the rewriting of early modern history.

The Early Modern Englishwoman: A Facsimile Library of Essential Works is one of the developments of this energetic reappraisal of the period. As the names on our advisory board and our list of editors testify, it has been the beneficiary of scholarship in the field, and we hope it will also be an essential part of that scholarship's continuing momentum.

The Early Modern Englishwoman is designed to make available a comprehensive and focused collection of writings in English from 1500 to 1750, both by women and for and about them. The three series of *Printed Writings* (1500–1640, 1641–1700, and 1701–1750) provide a comprehensive if not entirely complete collection of the separately published writings by women. In reprinting these writings we intend to remedy one of the major obstacles to the advancement of feminist criticism of the early modern period, namely the limited availability of the very texts upon which the field is based. The volumes in the facsimile library reproduce carefully chosen copies of these texts, incorporating significant variants (usually in appendices). Each text is preceded by a short introduction providing an overview of the life and work of a writer along with a survey of important scholarship. These works, we strongly believe, deserve a large readership—of historians, literary critics, feminist critics, and non-specialist readers.

The Early Modern Englishwoman also includes separate facsimile series of *Essential Works for the Study of Early Modern Women* and of *Manuscript Writings*. These facsimile series are complemented by *The Early Modern Englishwoman 1500–1750: Contemporary Editions*. Also under our general editorship, this series will include both old-spelling and modernized editions of works by and about women and gender in early modern England.

New York City
2003

INTRODUCTORY NOTE

An Epitome of the History of Faire Argenis and Polyarchus is Judith Man's English translation of a 1623 French work by Nicolas Coeffeteau, *Histoire de Poliarque et d'Argenis*, which is itself an abridgement and translation of one of the most widely read fictional works of the seventeenth century, John Barclay's 1621 Latin romance *Argenis*. An extended political allegory of the rise to power of the French king Henri IV, Barclay's romance is peppered by numerous veiled anecdotes of politics at the English and other European courts and long disquisitions on statecraft and political ethics. As a consequence of Barclay's subject matter and his decision to write in Latin, it has usually been assumed that he was addressing a learned and strictly male audience, but Man's translation is evidence that women did in fact read *Argenis*, and might even suggest that allegorical romance offered women writers and readers an inroad into political discourse. Epitome and translation, moreover, are both methods of interpretation, ways to revise and comment on a text and to bring it to bear on historical moments outside of its original context. This volume, in the hopes of providing a condensed glance at how romance, translation, and epitome function for one early modern woman writer, brings the complete text of Man's translation together with three appendices: the concluding episode from Coeffeteau's abridgement, and that same episode, in its much more elaborate original form, from both the second, London edition of Barclay's romance and the English translation of Barclay with which Man was most likely to have been familiar.

Judith Man

Nothing is known of Man beyond the details that she gives us in the prefatory material to her *Epitome*. She indicates that at Christmas 1639, when she made the translation, she was an eighteen-year-old gentlewoman and a member of the household of Thomas Wentworth, who as Lord Deputy of Ireland was one of the most powerful politicians in England and had just been created Earl of Strafford. We know of a Peter Man who was family solicitor for Thomas Wentworth and his father before him; Judith Man is not enumerated as one of his children in either his or his wife Dorothy's will, but it is possible she was a granddaughter or other relative. In her address to the reader of her *Epitome*, Man tells us that she traveled in France with her parents as a child and that she was an English Protestant. Probably in 1639 she was a companion to Wentworth's daughters Arabella, ten, and Anne, twelve.

An Epitome of the History of Faire Argenis and Polyarchus

Man's translation was printed early in 1640, in octavo, by E. Griffin for Henry Seile, almost certainly as a compliment to Strafford and an assertion of monarchical power in politically volatile times. The text is exceedingly rare, surviving in only two known copies, and has not been reprinted. Its title page mentions neither John Barclay nor Man herself by name, but gives prominent place to two other people: Nicolas Coeffeteau, Bishop of Marseilles, who 'extracted' from the Latin original his *Histoire de Poliarque et d'Argenis*, Man's source text; and Lady Anne Wentworth, elder daughter of the new Earl and the dedicatee of Man's book. Any description of Man's *Epitome* must deal with these two figures, but their significance becomes clear only after an account of John Barclay's *Argenis*.

John Barclay came to the court of James I from France with his father William, a Scottish professor of law at Louvain and a polemicist on the side of monarchy in the important Counter-Reformation debate over whether the Pope or the monarch should have supreme political and moral power in any given state. The younger Barclay stayed in England for almost a decade, as Gentleman of the King's Bedchamber, diplomat, and occasional polemicist himself. In 1616 he left the English court for Rome, where he wrote the multi-volume *Argenis* and died just before it was published. 'Argenis' is an anagram of the Latin 'Regina', or 'queen', with an 's' tacked on to the end, perhaps to indicate its roots in Greek romance as well; the title's allusion to such works as Machiavelli's *The Prince* should alert us that it is meant to be read as a treatise on statesmanship as much as a romance about love. Its publication created a sensation in Europe and England, because of its topicality, its hybrid nature, and what was judged to be its excellent Latin, and in the following decade it went through 24 Latin editions. Before 1700 it had seen 20 more Latin editions, translation into at least 13 languages, three continuations, and at least two adaptations for the stage, and it continued to be popular for at least another century. (Coleridge, to mention only one example, read and annotated it with enthusiasm.) In England James I commissioned Ben Jonson to translate it, but although Jonson's *Argenis* was entered in the Stationers' Register it was apparently destroyed before publication, in the fire that burned Jonson's library in 1623. English translations before Man's that did make it into print include one by Kingsmill Long, in 1625, and another by Robert Le Grys, which was commissioned by Charles I in 1628, during the controversy over the Petition of Right, perhaps because of the romance's support for monarchical power.

Barclay's romance, almost 500 folio pages long, tells of the crisis presented by the marriage of Princess Argenis of Sicily, whose fate as the only child of the weak King Meleander will determine the succession of the throne. The romance begins *in medias res*, with the arrival of the Mauritanian prince Archombrotus on Sicilian soil. Argenis has already fallen in love with the French prince Poliarchus, whose story is told in a series of flashbacks: cross-dressed as a princess in order to gain access to Argenis, he had been on hand to foil her abduction by a wicked courtier, and afterwards had declared his true identity and his love to Argenis, although not to her father. Almost as soon as Archombrotus arrives in Sicily the two princes find themselves in bitter rivalry, and shortly they also face competition from King Radirobanes of Sardinia. After a succession of wars, feuds, and dirty tricks, Meleander's throne is finally secured when Queen Hyanisbe, aunt to Archombrotus, reveals by means of some secret documents that her nephew is really Meleander's long-lost son. Having vanquished all other rivals, Poliarchus and Archombrotus realize that they can now 'share' Argenis – that is, they can divide up the property that she brings without war or bitterness.

Interspersed between episodes of this complicated plot are numerous learned conversations among courtiers, on subjects ranging from the inadequacy of astrology as a guide to politics to the proper relations between Parliament and monarch. Through his mouthpiece, the courtier Nicopompus, Barclay tells us that he has newly attempted to combine fiction with fact and delight with learning. The many 'keys' published with translations of the romance explain that Argenis herself stands for the French throne, and Poliarchus and Archombrotus together for Henri IV of France. Hanging on this central allegory are many smaller ones – stories of disputes between church and monarch, diplomatic missions gone wrong, even sexual misadventures among courtiers. Nicopompus informs us that this kind of truth – history veiled by fiction – is meant to pull readers into the story, so that they will recognize their own implication in the plot and thus be in a position to be educated by the 'real' truth in the romance, its moral and political lessons.

Barclay's romance fits into a number of Renaissance contexts. In its second book the Barclay-figure Nicopompus declares his intention to write a 'new kinde' of narrative, one in which some details are entirely fictional and others directly shadow events at European courts. This mixture of fiction with political allegory was undoubtedly the main reason for the romance's popularity, and it is also the reason why *Argenis* is now understood to be one of the primary ancestors of political romance in mid-century England. During the Civil War and Interregnum, Royalists produced long, complex accounts of the misadventures of princes, princesses and their courtiers that were also supposed to be read as explicit allegories of contemporary politics. (Among these romances are Roger Boyle's 1651 *Parthenissa*; the anonymous 1655 *Theophania*; Percy Herbert's *The Princess Cloria*, various installments of which were published through the 1650's; and the anonymous 1659 *Panthalia, or the Royal Romance*.) An ostensibly un-serious form, romance was a relatively safe way to popularize political dissent, and its interest in the personal, affective dimensions of authority made it an ideal argument for monarchy. *Argenis* is also probably a model, incidentally, for French heroic romance writers such as Madeleine de Scudéry, whose popularity in England is usually understood as a reason for the fad for English romance but who in fact may owe as much as she offers to English narrative traditions. *Argenis* cannot be said, of course, to be English, but after living a decade at James's court Barclay could hardly have been uninfluenced by English literary culture, and in fact one of the romance's greatest intellectual debts is to Philip Sidney's *Arcadia*. Along with the first part of Mary Wroth's *Urania*, also published in 1621, which is less overtly political but employs the same roman à clef structure, *Argenis* reprises *Arcadia*'s fascination with weak monarchs, incest as political metaphor, and the role of romance in the discourse of state. Sidney's own models were diverse: Italian romance such as Sannazaro's *Arcadia* and Tasso's *Gerusalemme Liberata*, Montemayor's Spanish *Diana*, ancient Greek romances such as Heliodorus's *Ethiopian History*, and in addition, perhaps, medieval verse romance, which in England, as Ann Astell has recently suggested, was probably part of a long tradition of political allegory in romance form. Modern critics and those contemporaries of Barclay who agreed that his was a new kind of writing are not wrong to see *Argenis* as the prototype for a kind of self-conscious allegory that would become endemic in mid-century political romance, but Barclay's work should also be seen as part of a long European tradition which had most recently been channeled through the English *Arcadia*.

At the same time, *Argenis* also belongs to a wide-ranging neo-Latin European intellectual culture. Throughout the sixteenth and the early part of the seventeenth centuries about one in ten books published in England was in Latin, most for the educational market. That the second Latin edition of *Argenis* (the edition from which the selection in this volume is reproduced) was published in London reflects both the work's great popularity in England and also, probably, the feeling that in some sense, given Barclay's time at the English court, it was English itself. Through the first half of the seventeenth century the most intellectually serious and scholarly books were still published in Latin, and booksellers imported a large number of these books from the Continent to satisfy the scholarly market. Romance was generally understood as a popular form, and 'Latin romance' might be seen in this period as a contradiction in terms. Barclay's decision to write in Latin was thus a bid for intellectual seriousness as well as for a large international readership. (It is no coincidence, of course, that *Argenis* fell out of critical fashion just when Latin stopped being the language of international scholarship.) Part of that scholarly readership was Nicolas Coeffeteau, bishop of Dardania and then Marseilles in France and a polemicist for papal and ecclesiastical over political authority. It is not clear why Coeffeteau decided to translate and abridge *Argenis*; he and Barclay shared a close mutual friend, Nicolas Claude Fabri, Seigneur de Peiresc, who was an attaché of the French ambassador in London during Barclay's time there and helped shepherd *Argenis* through publication after Barclay's sudden death in 1621, and perhaps Coeffeteau thought he was performing a labor of loyalty, if not love, by popularizing Barclay's work now that the other writer was no longer able to do so. Or perhaps his motives were opportunistic: instead of paying homage, he could have intended to expunge the romance's controversial digressions in order to counteract further popularization, at least in France, of ideas with which he disagreed. Whatever the reason, he radically reduced the size of the romance – from about 500 folio pages to 174 in tiny 32° – by removing all but the skeleton of the plot, and he also eliminated the flashbacks and the opening *in medias res* to make the narrative a straight linear one.

Coeffeteau does not call his work an epitome, but Man's interpretation of it as such suggests that the English version may also have affiliations with the large number of Continental neo-Latin epitomes of scholarly works, a genre that flourished as Latin education became more widespread. Roger Ascham, in his well-known educational treatise *The Schoolmaster* (1570), denounces epitomes for undervaluing the power and beauty of language (the assumption is that epitomes preserve only 'matter', or content) and promoting the loss of classic works in their original form. But he also makes the fascinating suggestion that epitomes, by toning down or eliminating what he calls excess rhetoric, produce temperance, and thus might be particularly useful for religious polemicists, who would produce more compelling arguments if they avoided 'spiteful railing'. Nicopompus himself argues that his allegorical technique will avoid 'railing', though his companions are skeptical. Perhaps Coeffeteau's decision to epitomize *Argenis* is also an attempt, given the culture of religious controversy in which both men wrote, to temper the polemic of a man to whom he was kindly inclined. This tempering function of epitome may, in turn, have been attractive to Man, who perhaps wished to avoid religious controversy either for reasons of decorum or from a desire to focus attention on other aspects of the romance. Her decision (or the printer's) to call her work an epitome may, lastly, also have been an attempt to meet the English appetite, evident from the moment Caxton began to print English books, for historical epitomes, abridged, schematic, and sometimes hugely popular renderings of the classical, religious, and national histories that served as sources for so much Renaissance literature.

As I suggested above, if for no other reason Man's *Epitome* would be important for indicating that women too read *Argenis*, thereby suggesting in turn that despite women's exclusion from the grammar-school education that would have taught them Latin, they were aware of and interested in this explicitly intellectual and political book and did have access to at least some of the scholarly and political culture surrounding the English and other international courts. But the *Epitome* has significance for many other reasons as well. Translation for Renaissance women was a kind of compromise, an avenue by which they could speak in the public arena without bringing upon themselves injunctions to silence and chastity. So, for instance, the hugely learned Mary Sidney, Countess of Pembroke, wrote little 'original' work of her own but translated both religious works (the Psalms, Philippe de Mornay's *A Discourse of Life and Death*) and secular ones (Robert Garnier's Senecan drama *The Tragedie of Antony*). (See Part 1, Vol. 6 of this series.) That translation was safer for women than other kinds of literary production, however, does not mean that it was insignificant; as recent work on translation theory has shown, the translator is never a simple conduit for a text but finds herself required to make interpretive decisions at every step. Man's *Epitome*, although almost entirely a word-for-word translation of Coeffeteau, is no exception. One of Man's few and most blatant revisions of her source is her title: where Coeffeteau called his abridgement the 'Histoire de Poliarque et d'Argenis', Man calls hers 'An Epitome of the History of faire Argenis and Polyarchus', switching the order of the protagonists (perhaps partly better to reflect Barclay's title, which was simply 'Argenis') and giving the princess an adjective. On the title page 'Argenis' is by far the largest word, followed in size by 'Epitome' and 'History' and then, another step smaller, 'Polyarchus'. In her dedication to Anne Wentworth, Man identifies Argenis with Anne, and the Stationer, in his address to the reader, takes this move one step further, depicting Argenis, Anne, and Man herself as the three Graces. It was usual for Barclay's readers to understand Poliarchus as Henry IV and Argenis as the prize for which he fought – monarchy, sovereignty, perhaps divine or popular sanction. The key printed with the 1636 edition of the English *Argenis* in fact identifies the rest of the characters with historical figures, then defines Argenis herself as 'a throne'. But Man clearly wants Argenis to be understood as an agent, like the rest of the romance's characters, perhaps for general ethical and philosophical reasons – to argue for female agency in history and politics – and perhaps also for the more historically particular reason that she wishes to be seen as an agent herself, even a political one. Probably the most significant decision Man made was to translate this romance in her particular place in time, and as a member of Strafford's household. Although we will probably never know for sure, it is more than possible that Man meant her translation as both compliment to and political justification of the Earl of Strafford – a possibility that makes even word-for-word translation something quite different from the simple 'diversion' she claims to be writing in her address to the reader.

If on the one hand Man's translation of a version of *Argenis* is an intervention in a scholarly and political culture that has typically been identified as masculine, on the other her decision to work with romance can be construed as conventionally feminine, for both good and ill. As a 'light' genre, romance is often identified in the medieval and Renaissance periods with women readers and writers, so that at least in this sense Man is not trespassing on masculine literary territory. At the same time, male readers frequently disparage romance for being frivolous, and by extension its women writers and readers for spending time on it; so, for instance, Edward Denny tells Mary Wroth, author of *Urania*, to 'leave idle bookes alone' and 'redeem the time with writing as large a volume of heavenly lays and holy love as you have of lascivious tales and amorous toys' (Roberts, xxxix). Denny is angry at Wroth here not only because she has dared to write a romance, but because the romance is also à clef, a story 'with a key' that figures real people and events in its fiction, and this connection between roman à clef and women is the final context that helps make sense of Man's topical, historically specific project in making and publishing her translation. *Urania* was not read as political allegory in the same way *Argenis* was, but its coded topicality and its deep interest, almost obsession, with the female writing self behind the fiction serve as models for later romance as surely as *Argenis* does. In this light Man's focus on Argenis herself starts to become interestingly complicated. Argenis's chief virtue in the *Epitome* is constancy in love (also the chief virtue of Wroth's heroine Pamphilia), which she sustains against opposition from her nurse, her other suitors, and her father. Royalist literature, from Caroline pastoral drama to Cavalier poetry to Interregnum prose romance, consistently uses romantic and erotic love as a metaphor for, sometimes even a means to, political loyalty to the monarch, and of course in so far as Argenis does convey with her the throne of France, her love for Poliarchus, and his for her, must by definition be political.

Likewise, translating a work that argues for constancy is for Man, as a member of the household of the Earl of Strafford in 1639, almost certainly a political act. Throughout the 1630's Wentworth served Charles I as Lord Deputy of Ireland, where he ruled with a famously iron hand. In July of 1639, faced with a deepening crisis over a rebellious Scotland, the king called him back to London, where Wentworth apparently underestimated the military effectiveness of the Scots and overestimated the sympathy of Parliament to both himself and Charles. His insistence that Charles must use 'extraordinary means rather than, by the peevishness of some few factious spirits, suffer his state and government to be lost', that in this desperate time the king must be 'loosed and absolved from all rules of government', intensified feelings in Parliament that he meant to put the king on the road towards military dictatorship, and by the early winter of 1639, when the king created him Earl of Strafford, he faced formidable opposition, both political and personal, in Parliament. (In November of 1639 Strafford was impeached by Parliament, and in the following spring, sacrificed to political inevitability by Charles, he was executed.) Strafford, says Man in her preface, is not a politician; he never 'asked or interceded' for the 'Pearled Crowne' that signifies his earldom, but rather was granted it for his 'good Services, being of the number of those of whome the French Proverbe makes mention, saying Tel demande assez, qui bien sert' (roughly, 'the best request for favor is good service'). Strafford is a man of action, not words; of convictions, not opportunities; his policies are driven not by any desire for self-aggrandizement but by his love for the king. In this context the *Epitome*'s emphasis on constancy in love may well be a compliment to Strafford and an admonition to his many opponents, and Man may be proclaiming her own loyalty, or that of her family, to Strafford and the king as well, perhaps for some preferment in marriage or other negotiations.

The appendices reproduce the closing chapters of Barclay's *Argenis*, from both the second, London edition of the Latin romance and Kingsmill Long's 1625 English translation, and the section from Coeffeteau's abridgement and translation which corresponds to these chapters. Coeffeteau preserves only a very small amount of the dialogue and monologue through which Barclay conveys most of *Argenis*'s plot and political philosophy; I have chosen to reproduce these sections from the end of the romance because the presence of the two extended soliloquies suggests that this is one of the rare moments that Coeffeteau found deserving of amplification. As will be clear on comparison of Barclay's original with Coeffeteau's and Man's abridgement, Argenis's monologue is Coeffeteau's entirely, and the emphasis on constancy as a moral (if not quite political) virtue finds echoes throughout the abridgements and also, fascinatingly, in other Jacobean and Caroline romance, most notably Wroth's *Urania*. (See Part I, Vol. 10 of this Series.) Other important differences suggested by comparison of these concluding sections include Coeffeteau's increased emphasis on character as a motivator of plot and the related marginalization, in the later versions, of political questions. Coeffeteau's decision to dispense with the elevated political prophecy at the very end of the romance and to conclude instead with a psychological truism is probably the abridgement's starkest illustration of these latter differences. As I suggested above, Man translates very literally from the French, frequently using cognates and preserving turns of phrase that are more French than English, but she is skilled enough that her translation never violates the sense of Coeffeteau's original.

Only two copies of the 1640 edition of Man's *Epitome* are known to be extant, one at the Bodleian Library at Oxford, which has been deemed too fragile for reproduction, and one at The Huntington Library, which is reproduced here. There are no other printed editions of the work. I have located only one copy of Coeffeteau's 1624 *Histoire de Poliarque et d'Argenis* (at the University of North Carolina at Chapel Hill) excerpts of which are reproduced here; other copies are known to survive in private collections in France. The work was reprinted in 1628, in substantially identical form. As noted above, Barclay's 1621 Latin *Argenis* was reprinted repeatedly throughout the seventeenth century and beyond. I have chosen to reproduce excerpts from the 1622 London edition because it would probably have been the most available to English readers. We have evidence from contemporary letters that the 1621 edition was very difficult to obtain at the English court, where it was much in demand, and probably the London edition was printed to meet this demand. A large number of copies of this edition survive in the United States and England, most in reproducible condition but most with a substantial amount of ink bleed-through because of the thinness of the paper. I have not entered into an exhaustive study of the surviving copies of this edition; most of the copies I surveyed being substantially the same, I have chosen to reproduce the second of the Folger Shakespeare Library's three copies. There are many variant readings in successive editions of the Latin *Argenis*; unfortunately, no one has yet prepared a critical edition or for that matter any modern edition, and there is no consensus about which of the many Latin editions is most authoritative nor how for this work authority might be defined. Finally, the English translation from which excerpts are reproduced is the second edition of Kingsmill Long's. This edition was printed in 1636, when Man was 14, and seems likely to have been the English edition she would have known, if she knew any. More significantly, her title page directly echoes the title page of this second edition in layout. In both the first and second editions the title runs, 'Barclay his Argenis, or the Loves of Polyarchus and Argenis'. In the first, 1625 edition of the Long translation, 'Barclay' is the largest word on the page, following which is, at about 2/3 the size, 'his Argenis, or the loves of', followed by, still smaller, 'Polyarchus and Argenis.' In 1636, perhaps because the fame of the characters had eclipsed the fame of the author, 'Barclay his Argenis' is substantially smaller than 'Polyarchus', which is by far the largest word on the page and substantially larger than 'Argenis' following. Man's title page reverses the positions of Polyarchus and Argenis, as noted above, but keeps the sizing, so that 'Argenis' becomes the largest word on the page – almost certainly an imitation of the earlier title page and possibly a suggestion that she or the printer considered the 1636 Long translation a direct antecedent. Both the 1636 English translation and Man's *Epitome* (as well as all the English editions of *Argenis* before 1636) were printed for Henry Seile, which might seem to suggest the printer's responsibility for the similar title pages, but Man herself claims responsibility for the reversal of 'Argenis' and 'Poliarchus' in her prefatory material. As with the Latin *Argenis*, many copies of the second edition of the Long translation survive throughout the United States and England, and there has never been any modern edition of Barclay in English. Again, I have not attempted anything like an exhaustive review of the extant copies of this edition of the translation but have reproduced excerpts from the Folger's adequate copy.

References

STC 1390 *Barclaii* [Barclay, 2nd edition] (1622)
STC 1396 *Epitome* [Man, tr.] (1640)
STC 1392.5 *Barclay* [Long, tr. 2nd edition] (1636)
Coeffeteau, Nicolas, tr. *Histoire de Poliarque et Argenis* (1624)

Astell, Ann (1999), *Political Allegory in Late Medieval England*, Ithaca: Cornell University Press
Barclay, John (1622, 1973), *Euphormionis Lusinini Satyricon*, tr. David A. Fleming, S.M., Nieuwkoop: B. De Graaf [contains substantial introductory material on Barclay]
Binns, J.W. (1990), *Intellectual Culture in Elizabethan and Jacobean England: The Latin Writings of the Age*, Leeds: Francis Cairns (Publications) Ltd.
Krontiris, Tina (1992), *Oppositional Voices: Women as Writers and Translators of Literature in the English Renaissance*, London: Routledge
Man, Dorothy, Will proved 14 March 1648, Borthwick Institute, York, England, located in bundle for March 1649–50
Man, Peter, Will proved 24 November 1637, Borthwick Institute, York, England, located in bundle for April 1638–9
Potter, Lois (1989), *Secret Rites and Secret Writing: Royalist Literature, 1641–1660*, Cambridge: Cambridge University Press
Roberts, Josephine A. (ed.) (1995), *The First Part of the Countess of Montgomery's Urania*. Binghamton: MRTS
Salzman, Paul (1985), *English Prose Fiction, 1558–1700: A Critical History*, Oxford: Clarendon Press
Smith, Nigel (1994), *Literature and Revolution in England 1640–1660*, New Haven: Yale University Press
Urbain, Charles (1894), *Nicolas Coeffeteau, Un des fondateurs de la prose française*, Lyon: Librairie Générale Catholique et Classique
Wheatley, Chloe (2001), 'Epitomes of Early Modern History', Ph.D. dissertation, Columbia University, New York

AMELIA A. ZURCHER

An Epitome of the History of Faire Argenis and Polyarchus (1640, *STC* 1396) is reproduced, by permission, from the copy at The Huntington Library (shelfmark 56660). The text block of the original measures 70×120 mm.

AN EPITOME

OF THE

HISTORY

OF FAIRE

ARGENIS

AND

POLYARCHUS,

Extracted out of the Latin, and put
in French, by that Great and
Famous Writer,
M. N. COEFFETEAV
Bishop of Marseilles.

And translated out of the French into
English by a yong GENTLEVVOMAN.

DEDICATED
To the Lady ANNE WENTVVORTH.

LONDON,
Printed by *E. G.* for *Henry Seile* at the Tygers
head in Fleetstreet. 1640.

TO THE
MOST VERTVOVS
MY MOST
HONORED LADY,
THE LADY
ANNE WENTWORTH,
Eldest Daughter
To the Right Honorable
the Earle of *Strafford*, Lord
Lieutenant of *Ireland.*

 *T is not needfull, I
should use many
words, to let You
know, that this Booke belongs.*

A 2   *to*

The Epistle

to Your Ladiship, *It suffi-*
cing that You know, I am
Yours, (*since You gave me*
the liberty, *to call my selfe so,*
when I had the Honour to bee
admitted into the House of my
Lord Your Father, *where*
my Parents did introduce me,
and where I have profited neere
You *and* my Lady Ara-
bella Your Sister, *as in a*
Schoole of Vertue) *whence it*
followes, that I onely give You
that which is Yours, *being*
found in me : *and though it*
should be otherwise, I could not
present

Dedicatory.

present it to any one, that deserved it better then Your selfe.

The reading of this Epitome,
MADAM, which I dedicate
unto You, as being Yours,
and which I put to light under
Your protection, will represent
ARGENIS unto You, as the
Fairest, most Vertuous, and
Constant Princesse of Her
time. And I have thought, reading this History, that I have
seene Your true portraiture in
the person of this Faire Lady. For, making a Parallell of
this Princesse with Your

A 3   Ho-

The Epistle

Honour *I finde* You *very suteable*; *yea* I *can witnesse with truth, that* You *surpasse* Her; *since that besides the* Beauty *of the* Body *wherewith* Nature *hath endowed* You; You *are also inrich'd with that of the* Soule *beyond measure*; *and as touching* Vertue *whereof* You *are a* Patterne, You *excell* Her, *being* Vertue *it selfe.* You *have besides the knowledge of the* True God, *which is the* Ground *and* Basis *thereof, and whereof our* Argenis *was ignorant*;

ignorant; *and as for* Constancy, You *have not* (*I dare say,*) Your *equall, seeing* You *are resolved, to be conformable unto the* Will *of* GOD, *and of my* Lord Your Father. *To which may bee added* Your Birth (*as well as unto our* ARGENIS) *which makes* You *truely worthy to beare the* Pearled Crowne, *where-with my* Lord Your Father *hath beene Honoured, without asking or intercession; but by the* Kings *onely* Will, *who gave it* Him *for* His e-

minent

The Epistle

minent *Vertue* and good *Services*; being of the number of those of whom the *French Proverbe* makes mention; saying, TEL DEMANDE ASSEZ, QUI BIEN SERT.

And to conclude MADAM, *I say, that even as it hath pleased* GOD, *to fill our* ARGENIS *with Joy and Consent, giving* Her, Her POLIARCHUS, *as the most Compleat* Prince of the Earth, He *may* send You for Your, *and* Your most Honourable Parents *Comfort*, a Husband

band *worthy of* You, *And I am confident,* Hee *will bee farre Compleater then* POLI-ARCHUS. *Theſe are the Wiſhes*

MADAM,

Of your moſt humble,

moſt affectionate,

moſt obedient, and

moſt obliged ſervant,

Judith Man.

To the Courteous Reader.

Gentle Reader, my humor inclining to Melancholy, induces me sometimes, to seeke in my Closet for some diversion, in the reading of Bookes, suteable to a Gentlewoman of my quality, and of eighteene yeeres of age; That is it wherein I have most perticularly applied my selfe this Christmas, and amongst the rest, in the reading of this Booke, which hath pleased me, not only for the subject whereof it treats, but also, comming from the hands of an Author, whose memory

mory I honor, though of a contrary Beliefe to mine, becaufe that
being in France, in my Parents
company, I have heard a great
efteeme to be made of him, as of
the moft learned Prelate of his
time. So as I might make my felfe,
fo much the more perfect, in the
French tongue, I refolved to tran-
flate it, for my owne particular
fatisfaction, having no other defigne, then to warme my felfe
therewith; as I have done with
fome others : But I could not
make this Worke fo fecretly, but
that thofe who watch over my
actions, and endeavour my diver-
fion, had notice thereof, by whom
I have beene in a manner forc'd
(leaft *I* fhould trangreffe againft
the

the Law of God) to expose it to
the publike view ; And all the
favour which *I* could obtaine,
hath beene to suffer mee to make
choice of a second ARGENIS,
under whose Protection *I* send it.
And J intreat thee, *Gentle Reader,* to oblige me so farre, as not
to presume that J doe it, out of
vanity ; because it is not without
example, and could produce thee
many of my sexe, who have traced
me the way, witnesse the translation into French of Sir *Philip Sidneys Arcadia,* the *New Amarantha,* and the *Vrania,* with many
others ; neither have I done it to
be spoken of, knowing very well,
that those of, my sexe, who are
least spoken of, are the more to
be

To the Reader.

bee efteemed : But onely have I done it by meere obedience and duty, therefore I pray thee to excufe the faults, if there be any, and remember, that women (for the moft part) are unacquainted with the ftudie of Sciences ; and by that meanes, may fooner erre; Alfo, I efteeme that thou art Courteous enough, to ufe mee according to the courtefie and cuftome, due to the Ladies of this Countrie, where I was borne ; And of whofe Priviledge I make ufe, giving ARGENIS the precedency, rather then unto POLIARCHVS in the Frontifpiee of this Booke; And in fo doing, I fhall not be a little obliged to thee.

J.M.

The Stationer to
the Reader.

Entlemen, *I should not hold my selfe satisfied with my Impression, if I did not tell you, that I hold it for a favour, in the beginning of this yeare, to see my Shop adorned with this little* Volume, *which comes from the hands of one of the most Vertuous, and Comeliest Gentlewomen of this Countrey, and which belies not her birth, which is truely Noble. And but that shee is full of respect and humility towards* ARGENIS,
and

and the *FAIRE LADY*, unto whom she hath Dedicated this Worke, they could make the most agreeable concordance, that could be seene; Also viewing them together (though with the eyes of the minde) I imagine I see the Graces, or those three Faire Goddesses, which puzzled so much, that Judge of Beauty. And therefore I desire You Gentlemen, to esteeme it, as this reputation merits, that you may not but applaud her, to the end that hereafter, she may make you partakers of her lucubrations; and in case you finde any faults, attribute them unto the Printer, for they are his, as proceeding from the Impression. God preserve you.

THE

THE
HISTORY
OF FAIRE
ARGENIS
AND
POLIARCHUS
EPITOMIZ'D.

ORTUNE proud and insolent, beyond all imaginationd, emands a sumptuous Theater, to cause the might of *Her Empire*, to appeare. It is in the *Court* of Great *Kings*, where *She* elevates the Trophies of *Her* tyranny, & where *She* brandishes *Her* vanity. It is there that *She* takes delight, to breake a *Scepter* afunder, to overthrow a *Crowne*, and to tread under

B foot

foot, all this pride of the earth, to the end *She* might render *Her* victories, so much the more glorious by such magnificent ruines, and *Her* Trophies the more illustrious, by such noble spoiles. But if amongst those Tragick accidents, *She* doth afford some cause of contentment, *She* doth temper it with so much bitternesse, that ordinarily, there is more prickles then Roses found in *Royalty*. This *History* is a lively portraiture therof, and causes us to see remarkable examples in it.

Meleander King of Sicily, possessing a rich State, and seeing himselfe adored by *His* subjects, who tasted with an extraordinary delight, the mildnesse of *His* government, thought to be arrived at the height of *His* glory. And that *He* might say he was happy on all sides, *He* was *Father* of a *Daughter* so accomplished in all kinds of perfections, that those who saw *Her*, imagined that *Heaven* had assembled all the treasures of beauty, and gathered all the riches of comlinesse, to forme this lofty *Master-*

peece

peece of nature. *He* imagined that this yong *Sunne*, should be the ornament of his *Crowne*, the prop of his *State*, the delight of his *Life*, and the confolation of his *Old age*. But men are ignorant of their deftinies, and know not what may befall them. The event then, made *Him* know, that as the greateft lights are fubject unto the greateft fhadows, fo the greateft profperities are expofed unto the greateft accidents, therefore one muft not fo much truft unto the favours of *Fortune*, but that one muft dread *Her* inconftancy.

Argenis then was the name of the *Heire of Sicily*, which ought to be as a living fpring of all goodnefle to *Her Father* and *Her State*, fees *Her* felfe to be the fubject of a furious and bloody warre, raifed by a *Prince*, one of *Meleander's* fubjects, who having had the temerity, to aske *Her* in marriage, received the refufall which his prefumption merited. The image of this contempt, made fuch a furious impreffion upon this wilde and ambitious fpirit, that to

B 2 take

take revenge, hee refolved to put the
Father out of the world, and to fteale
away the *Daughter* to crowne his parricide. This execrable defigne had come
to paffe, if the *Divinity*, which hath a
fpeciall care of *Crownes*, and which loves
Kings, had not miraculoufly put by, the
misfortune whereof the *Sicilian Scepter*
was threatned.   All *Europe*, and *Affrick*
alfo were filled with the rumor of *Argenis*'s beauty, which was placed amongft
the wonders of the world and nature.
A thoufand yong couragious fpirits,
taken with *Her* love, had refolved to
ferve *Her*, and to imploy all their induftry and valour, to infinuate themfelves
in *Her* favour. Amongft the reft *Polar-
chus Prince of France*, and *Heire* of one of
the faireft *Crownes* in the world, fuffe-
ring *Himfelfe* to bee tranfported with
this paffion, fought out for this glory
with more fucceffe then wifedome.
(But ought one to looke for any in
love?) Imagining in *Himfelfe* that an
extraordinary beauty merited no common purfuits ; *Hee* left his *Kingdome*,
and

and taking a *Gentlewomans* habit, croſſed
the ſea, and went to *Sicily*, where *He* in-
formed *Himſelfe* diligently of the place
where the *Princeſſe* was, to whom *He*
deſired, with ſo much paſſion to offer
His ſervice. *Meleander* fearing leaſt de-
ſpaire ſhould cauſe *Lycogenes* to procure
ſome ſhame unto *Her*, had placed *Her* in
a ſtrong Hold, where *She* paſſed the
time with *Her* maids, being viſited of
none but *Her Father*, who ſometime
going from *Syracuſe* (which was not
farre from thence,) came to ſee *Her*, and
ſtayed with *Her* to divert *Himſelfe* in
Her company. *Poliarchus* following *His*
deſigne, goes that way, and ſpying the
meanes, to enter in this agreeable ſoli-
tarineſſe, takes *His* journey towards *Syracuſe*, where being arrived *He* finds
by good fortune *Seleniſſa Argenis ſes*
Governeſſe within the *Temple of Iuno*,
where *She* was at *Her* devotions. He
had learn'd in what ranke ſhe was with
the *Princeſſe*. *He* cals her aſide, and having caſt *Himſelfe* at her feet, beſeeches
her to take pitty on the moſt unfortu-

nate *Lady* which the Sunne shined on,
on earth, and to give *Her* the meanes to
tell *Her* some thing, which could not be
knowne to any but she, unto whom *She*
brought letters from a great *Princesse.*
The *Strangers* comely behaviour, the
novelty of *Her* habit, and *Her* language,
which shewed *She* was not of the *Court
of Sicily,* caused in *Selenissa* a desire to
learne what *She* would say. Then going
out of the throng, *She* leads *Her,* to her
sisters house, and entred alone in a
Closet fit to receive *Her* most secret
thoughts.   Then *Poliarchus* kissing the
letters gives them unto *Her,* and at last
leads so happily this enterprize, that *He*
causes himselfe to be taken for a *French
Princesse,* which the rage of *Her Vncle*
had driven into *Sicily* to looke out for
the refuge and surety, which *She* could
not finde in *Her Realme* amongst *Her*
friends.   My name, said *he,* is *Theocrine
the Kings daughter, and Sister unto the
Heire of the Crowne of France,* whom this
parricide (who hath procured all my
mis-fortunes,) hath caused to be poiso-
ned

ned that hee might usurpe his *Diadem.*
That which made her to give more
faith unto his words, was, that calling
a Freed slave who gave *Her* a Cabinet,
which *She* had committed to his charge,
she drew forth the most exquisite riches, and the fairest precious stones, that
were ever seene in *Europe*; then with a
magnificence which truely resembled
a great *Princesse*, gave such a great number unto *Selenissa*, that at the instant
(suffering her selfe to bee dazled with
their sparkling and radiation) *she*
bound her selfe with a strong tye of
affection unto *Poliarchus*, which she took
for *Theocrine.* Whereupon *Theocrine*
conjured her to embrace *Her* affaires,
and to procure that favour towards *Ar-*
genis, that *she* might receive *Her* into
Her company, where *She* pretended not
to hold the ranke of a *Princesse*, but
would esteeme her selfe happy to hold
the quality of a *Waiting-woman.*

Selenissa being touch'd with *Her* complaints, offers *Her* all manner of assistance, neverthelesse, said she unto *Her*,

to give you accesse in the *Princesses* house, is a thing which is not in my power, by reason of the strict defence, which the King hath made, not to suffer any strangers of either sexe to see *Her*. But *Theocrine*, who desired noting more, then to enjoy this glory, conjures her to breake this obstacle, and to mediate this favour towards the *King*, with whom *She* doubted not, but shee was powerfull, since *He* had committed to her trust that which *He* held most deare in the world, the *Princesse his daughter*. Being overcome by such charming intreaties, shee undertakes to enforme *Meleander* of this, whom *She* soone after caused to yeeld, telling *Him* al the good which shee could invent of this faire *Stranger*. At her returne, she declares unto *Argenis*, the occasion of her journey, & makes *Her* so favorable a report of the beauty, comlinesse, and magnificence of *Theocrine*, that *She* offers not onely to receive *Her* as a great *Princesse*, but also to love *Her* as *Her Sister*. Being then inflamed, with a desire to see *Her*,
the

she commands that without any farther delay, *she* should be brought in, that *she* might see if *Her* presence would equall the glorious praises which were giuen *Her. She* is then where *she* desires. At this first enterview, *She* forgets nothing of *Her* good behaviour, allurements, and attractive lookes, to charme the *Princesses* heart, who begins to bee but one *Soule* with *Hers. She* can so artificially accommodate *Her* humour unto that of *Argenis*, that in a short time *She* doth purchase a full power over *Her* mind, though not in the same quality which *She* wished. They then, passed away the time so sweetly toge ther, that they thought they were in Heavens glory. But *Licogenes*, unto whō the remembrance of the injury, which he thought to have received, gave him cruell torments, raised a tempest which troubled the calme of their delights. For, having plotted with his friends, the meanes to revenge himselfe, the resolution of this infamous counsell was, that the *Fort* ought to be

surprised

surprifed, to make away the *King*, and take perforce from thence the *Heire of the Kingdome*, and fo put himfelfe in quiet poffeffion of the *Crowne*; that, to differre any longer, it would br the way to ruinate their affaires, confidering the accidents which might happen. Therefore that hee fhould fhew himfelfe a man, and that hee fhould finde in them the fuccour and affiftance, which hee could hope for, of thofe who had a whole intereft in his trouble. There needed not, to make ufe of ftronger reafons, to perfwade a fpiric already imbrued with this crime.

It was long, fince *Licogenes* faw with griefe the *Scepter of Sicily* in the hands of *Meleander*. But to bring this furious counfell to paffe, hee thought it fit to corrupt certaine Souldiers, who fhould know the entrances of this Fortreffe. He finds out one, who being conquered by his promifes, offers to fulfill his defire, fo that hee procure him confederates whofe courages may bee like his, and declares unto him, that hee knew
the

the meanes to enter, by the Sea fide
where there was no guard. *Licogenes*
glad to have found fuch a fit inftru-
ment for his perfidioufneffe, gives him
conforts as defperate as he, and as refolute to commit a parricide. Upon a
night then, that *Meleander* was arrived
there, to disburden (according to *His*
wonted ufe) fome part of his forrowes
in *His daughters* bofome; thefe traitors
knew how to follow their enterprife fo
well, that they entred into the *Fort*, and
having feparated themfelves in two
bands, went the one to the *Kings* lodgings, and the other to the *Princeffes.*
Argenis thought on nothing elfe, but
fweetly to paffe away the time, amongft
Her Ladies, and caufed *Selexiffa* and
Theocrine (whofe beds were in her
chamber) to entertayne *Her* with a
thoufand pleafant difcourfes: *Meleander*
whofe age tooke away the fweetneffe
of this entertainment, had retired himfelfe to take reft. *Argenis* underftan-
ding a noife, which *She* was not us'd to
heare, holds up *Her* eyes, and feeing fo
many

many armed men to enter thronging in one after another, is frighted, and begins to cry out with feare. *Her* other Ladies surprized with the like astonishment, shew no more assurance, and for all their defence, have recourse to their teares. But the gentle *Theocrine* perceiving one, (who had advanced himselfe first) to lay hands on the *Princesse,* lets the reines loose to *Her rage,* and with an extraordinary courage, layes hold on that traytors sword, wreathes it from him, and presently employes it, against him from whom *She* had taken it, and layes him dead in the place. Then taking up his buckler, *She* runnes upon the rest of these rascals, whereof *she* cuts some part in pieces, and causes the rest to looke out for the doore. Another band of the conjurors, had rush'd in *Meleanders* chamber, whom having found asleepe in *His* bed, there needed no great strength to seaze on *Him.*

Theocrine, who had none left to fight with, hearing the noise, which those wicked

wicked rogues made about the *King*, went that way, and entring in the chamber, perceived a spectacle which would have drawne teares from a Tyger. Those infamous *Hang-men* had bound this great *King* with cords, and loaded *Him* with chaines, who amongst so much insolence and brutality, perceiv'd before *His* eyes nought else, but the images of despaire and horrour. The sorrow to see the *Father* of *Her Argenis* so unworthily abused, swells *Her* courage in such sort, that without any feare of danger where *She* was going to precipitate *Her selfe*, *She* enters upon these desperate fellowes, and having made a cruell slaughter amongst them, addresses *Her selfe* unto *Meleander*, and taking away the cords and chaines, said these few words unto *Him*. SIR, *Those who have committed this outrage against you, have not kept the respect due unto* Scepters, *and your vertue. But the Gods have given me the grace to put you againe in case, to make an exemplary punishment, of the authors of this barbarous attempt. Arme*

your selfe, I am going to take order about
the rest of your affaires; for it is to
be feared, least those who have had the au-
dacity, to plot so infamous a treason should
make a last attempt, to asswage their rage,
which will not be thus ended.   At the instant *Theocrine* gives a generall allarum,
and gives notice to the Guard, of their
fault, and of the danger wherein the
King had lately beene.   And as *She saw*
Meleander's safety to be made sure, *she*
came unto her *Argenis,* and kneeling on
the ground, us'd this language.   Faire
Princesse, *it is bootlesse now to dissemble,*
any longer; the miracles of your beauty, have
given strength to my arme, to take revenge
for the cruell injury , which hath beene done
to the Sicilian Scepter.   *I am not a* Lady,
as hitherto you have believed. I also esteeme,
that, what you have seene mee performe, hath
already dis-abused you.   At least, *it is im-*
possible, that henceforth, Meleander *should*
take me to be, what hee thought I was.   For
feare then, least I should ruinate my designes,
instead of advanceing of them , I take my
leave of you : But before I goe from the pre-
sence

sence of your faire eyes, I most humbly desire
you, by all the graces, whereof Heaven hath
so richly endowed you, to pardon mee this
offence, which is an effect of the power of
Love, unto which the Gods themselves cannot resist. You have prostrate at your feet,
the Heire of the Crowne of France, who
begs pardon of you. My name is Poliarchus, and not Theocrine. I have borrowed
this, that I might enter where Poliarchus
could not have had accesse: I part from you
with the same sorrow, that I should part
with my life: but I hope that by my services
I shall open the way to more liberty. Pro-
nounce my sentence, and I will take it from
you, even as the conquered, receives it from
the Conquerour.

Argenis being, as it were, thunder-
struck, by the freedome of these words,
finds Herselfe surprised, and at the same
instant, hath an inward combat by two
severall passions, of Love and Feare,
which held Her soule in agitation, in
such sort that being astonied at Theocrines language, She knowes not what
answere to make Him. Feare, that this
action

action fhould make a fpot, in *Her Glory*,
caufes *Her* at firft, to breath forth fome
fparkles of Choler.   *She* complaines of
this audacity, and fhewes *She* doth not
approve thofe fictions, whereby *she*
might receive more blame,   then the
Author could expect contentment. Nevertheleffe, at laft *Love*, that (fo many
prefent victories went fortifying) bani-
fhes all thofe *Feares*, and caufes *Her* to
finde *Theocrines* excufes good,to whom
at that time *She* doth in few words dif-
clofe *Her* thoughts, and teftifies unto
Him, that thofe proceedings are not dif-
pleafing to *Her*, but enjoynes *Him* to
publifh *His* fexe, and to make himfelfe knowne, to be the valiant *Poliar-*
chus.

This generous *Prince*, who onely
fought triumphs to infinuate *Himfelfe*
by *His* valour, into *Argenis's* favour,re-
affumes the name of *Poliarchus*, and at
the fame time, kiffing *His Miftreffes* faire
hands, goes out of the *Fortreffe* and
fteales away from *Meleander*, and *His*
Guard, bufied in the feeking out of the
                                        factious,

factious, whereof they made a horrible
slaughter. In the meane time the *King* is
troubled to finde out the Author of *His*
liberty, and as *His Daughter* tels *Him*
that *He* is obliged of *His* life, unto *Theo-*
crine, *He* desires to see *Her*, that *He*
might give *Her* the praises, and recom-
pence due to so eminent, and prodigious a vertue.   But being inform'd that
she is vanish'd, as a lightning, and that
she is not to bee found, *He* presently
imagines, that doubtlesse, *she* was no
mortall creature, but the *Goddesse Pallas*,
who foreseeing his misfortune, had taken the forme of this Lady, to put by
the ruines of *Sicily*, which was in *Her*
keeping. Thereupon, even as supersti-
tion is fertile in new devotions, *He* re-
volves with himselfe, with what new
tribute of piety, *He* may repay, this remarkable good deed, which seemed to
be beyond all manner of retribution:
and wandring in *His* thoughts, *He* caused the *Chiefest* of *His Counsell* to be assembled, unto whom speaking of this
adventure, *He* testified to owe *His* life

C   and

and safety, to a particular assistance of
the *Divinity*, rather then to any mans
succour, letting them know thereby,
that *He* had a designe to erect new ho-
nours and worship, unto the *Goddesse*
unto whom *He* imagined to be indebted, for *His* miraculous preservation.
Such a Religious design having beene
greatly applauded and approved by
the common voices of all the *Counsell*;
Meleander whose soule was already full
of these religious thoughts, and who
feared, that shewing *Himselfe* ungratefull towards the *Gods*, *He* should oblige
them, to draw backe their blessings
from *His Crowne*, was easily led away
with this advice, and calling *His Daughter*, opens *His* deliberation unto *Her*,
and perswades *Her*, so artificially, that
She freely accepted, the quality of *Mi-
nervas High Priest*, in acknowledge-
ment of the favour which *she* had
shewed, to *Her Father* and *State*. There
She is then wholly tyed, to the *Goddesses*
service, by vertue of *Her* new Office, now
She thinks on nothing else then the or-
dering

dering of the facrifices, and ruling of the holy ceremonies.

In the meane time *Lycogenes*, who knowes his crime to be unpardonable, affembles his friends, reprefents unto them, that their fafety confifts in hoping none, and that they muft come to an open force, fince craft and artificiall cunning have not fucceeded. And whereas the horror of this offence, fhould have caufed the armes to have fallen from his hands, hee prepares to give battayle unto his *King*. His felony gives meanes unto the *French Prince*, to caufe *His* great courage to appeare, afwell under the name of *Poliarchus*, as it had done, under that of *Theocrine*. He had gone and prefented *Him* elfe unto *Meleander* as being newly arrived in *His Court*, not making *Himfelfe* knowne to be *Him*, who had newly faved *His Life* and *State*. He had beene received there as a ftranger, and in few dayes, had left both to the *King*, and all the *Court*, a great opinion of *His* valour. During that time, *He* found the meanes often-

C 2   times,

times, to fee, *His Argenis*, amongſt the
ſacrifices, which were rendred unto
Minerva, for *Theocrines* victory. Neither
His, nor *Argenis's* devotion, was not ſo
much fixt, on the contemplation of the
ceremonies nor on the admiration of
all the pompe, as to enterchange amorous lookes, wherein lay all their felicity.

The envious army, which was already in the field, troubled all this ſolem-
nity, and oblig'd the *King* to take up
Armes, to oppoſe the fury of the rebels.
He had a ſingular confidence in *Poliarchus His* valour, which belyed not this
hope, nor the good opinion which the
world had conceived of the greatneſſe
of *His* courage. The two Armies being
in ſight, *He* began the fight, and as a
mighty war-like thunder, unto which
nothing can reſiſt, did ſo much by the
wonders of *His* ſword, that *Meleander*
won a glorious victory, and put the rebels out of hopes, to attempt any more,
the hazzard of Combats. Diſpaire made
them ſeeke after peace; they have per-
miſſion,

miffion, to fend their *Deputies* in *Court*, to make the overture of fome treaty. *Poliarchus*, who could not live in reft, at the firft newes of this peace, which *He* did not approve, not believing, that the *King* ought to truft to *Traytors*; refolved to goe elfewhere, to finde out new occafions of *Glory*. Having then left the *Court*, and traverfing a great foreft, having no other thoughts then on *His Argenis*, which filled all *His* fpirits; *Hee* meets thofe whom *Licogenes* fent unto *Meleander*, rather ecquipped like *Cavaleers*, or to fpeake the truth like *Robbers*, then *Ambaffadours*. They immediately knew *Him* for the Author of their misfortune, and enraged, with fury, refolve to revenge on *Him* the affront, which *His* valour caufed them to receive. At the fame time, they fet on *Him*, and make it appeare, that they would bereave *Him* of *His* life. But *He*, who could feare nothing, not being aftonied, at their threates, makes them feele the effects of *His* courage, overthrowes two, dead upon the place,

fcatters

ſcatters the others, and puts them to flight. Thoſe that could eſcape, goe and fill the *Court* with their complaints, and aggravate this outrage, done unto *Am-baſſadors*, whoſe perſons are held for *ſa-cred*, yea amongſt the *Barbarous*. They demand Juſtice which cannot be denied them, becauſe the *Court* hath no know-ledge of their crime, nor of the inno-cence, of *Him*, whom they accuſed. It is true, that *Meleander* could not ima-gine, that ſo notorious a villany, could have entred, in ſo noble a courage, and beſides all that, that which came from *Licogenes'es* party was to bee ſuſpected, alſo the Souldiers whol-ly affected to *Poliarchus*, who in their ſight, had done ſo many wonders in the *Field*, did openly jeere at this ac-cuſation, which, in what kind ſoever, it could be interpreted; could not, but turne, to the ſhame of thoſe, who made it, ſince they accuſed, one man alone, to have beaten five, well armed, and in caſe to defend themſelves. But, the conjurors faction, was ſo puiſſant, in

Court ; that, at laſt, it obtained that *Poli-archus*, ſhould be condemned, and to be deſtined, to ſerve for a ſacrifice, unto the *Kings* enemyes fury, who in defending of *Him*, might have cauſed a ſuſpition, amongſt thoſe diffident ſpirits, that *He* had done nothing, but by *His* authority. Order is then given every where to take *Him*, and alſo, the Commons are armed, to the end, that all meanes of eſcaping, might bee taken away.

In the meane time, it hapned during the fight, that, *Archombrotus Prince of Mauritania*, who was alſo ſearching out adventures, under a diſguiſed habit, was by chance, neere the place, where the combat was given. *He* was newly landed, (having beene beaten with ſundry tempeſts at ſea) neere unto that great and thicke Foreſt, where *He* was gone, thinking to take ſome reſt under the ſhade of ſome trees, being wearied of the ſea. But the vertuons *Timoclea*, who had ſeen the furious outrage, done to the *Prince of France*, came unto *Him*

C 4   weeping.

weeping and waking *Him*, conjured
Him, that if *He* would doe an action,
worthy the generofity which appeared
in *His* vifage , that without any further
delay, *He* fhould goe and fuccour the
moft valiant man in the world, that
Robbers endeavoured to murther. Opening *His* eyes , *He* fearches for *His* Armour confufedly, and preparing *Himfelfe*, at all adventures , endeavours to
put *Himfelfe* in cafe to fight. *Timoclea*
fearing, leaft the number, might op-
preffe valour, urges *Him* to advance,
and reprefents unto *Him* the neceffity,
and danger , wherein *Poliarchus* finds
Himfelfe. *He* who was enflamed with
defire, to have *His* courage to appeare,
in fo faire an occafion, without further
delay, fpurres *His* Horfe towards the
place of the combat. But *He* fees, with
fome kind of forrow, that *He* arrives too
late, and that *He*, whom *He* is defirous
to fuccour, hath needed no other affiftance, then that, of *His* fword. Ravifh'd
with this wonder, *He* doth accoft *Him*,
and having courteoufly faluted *Him*,
informes

informes *Himselfe* of the particulars of
this encounter, offers to aſſiſt *Him*, in
caſe there remaines any enemy, to fight
with, and conjures *Him*, to honour *Him*
ſo much, as to imploy *Him* in this quar-
rell. *Poliarchus* reſting extreamely ſa-
tisfied of the *Prince of Mauritania's* good
behaviour, and courteſy, thanks *Him* for
this freedome, and aſſures *Him* of the
eſteeme *Hee* makes of *His* courage, not
refuſing to make uſe of it, in caſe, *His*
affaires oblige *Him* thereunto. But,
Gentle Cavaleere, ſaid *He*, I know neither
thoſe, who have ſo cowardly aſſaulted
me, nor the reaſon of the furious hatred,
which they beare me. *Timoclea* arriving
thereupon with ſome of *Poliarchus His*
ſervants, breakes off the two *Princes*
diſcourſe, and taking the word conjures
them, to goe out of this Foreſt, and follow her, to a houſe which ſhee hath,
neere unto that place, where they might
learne the true cauſes of this encounter. They went then al together with
Timoclea, where they are hardly arrived,
when the Shepheards of the Country,

come

come to give them notice, that all the
champion, is full of kindled fires, every
where, and that doubtleffe, there is
fome accident fallen out at *Court*; feeing
that was never done, but upon great
and important occafions. And that *He*
might take no reft, news were brought,
that *Poliarchus* was the fubject of all
this emotion, to which they adde that
upon the *Ambaffadours* complaint, *He*
hath beene condemned in *Court*. *Poliarchus* feeing that 'tis *He*, whom this
tempeft threatens, breathes forth all
manner of outrages againft *Meleander*,
doth reproach *His* fervices, complaines
of *His* ungratitude, accufes alfo the innocent Starres, as if they were the caufe
of *His* mif-fortune. *Timoclea* fearing
leaft *He*(unto whom all *Sicily* owed their
fafety) fhould fall in the hands of thofe
Traitors, that they fhould advance *His*
ruine, by their artificiall deceits opens
Him the way, how to fhade *Himfelfe*,
againft this tempeft, fhewes *Him* at the
going out of a clofet, of *Her* houfe, a
long Vault, which went under ground,
whereof

whereof the avenewes, were knowne to
few, and conjures *Him* to make ufe of
this opportunity, not onely to fteale
away, from the eyes of thofe, who
fought *Him*, but alfo to goe out of *Sicily*
under the favour of a borrowed vifage,
wherewith fhe could fo artificially dif-
guife *Him*, that *His* moft intimate
friends, would hardly take *Him* to bee
Poliarchus. At laft, *He* is overcome
with her perfwafions, makes ufe of the
opportunity, which fhe prefents unto
Him, and though unwilling, confines
Himfelfe within this Vault, (untill he can
give fome order for *His* retreate) where
Timoclea, and the *Prince of Mauritania*,
would needs conduct *Him*, daring not
to truft thofe of the houfhold, whofe
faith they fufpected; having left *Him* in
this cave, and being come backe to the
houfe, *Timoclea* began to entertaine her
guefie, with the beft and moft civill difcourfes which fhe could invent. In the
meane time *Timoclea* and *Archombrotus*,
thinking to affure *Poliarchus His* life, did
almoft ruinate *His* affaires. To take
away

away all fufpition, they bethought thē-
felves, to caufe a rumor of *His* death, to
be fpread abroad, and that none might
doubt of it, caufed *His* fervants to be
feene, weeping the loſſe of their *Ma-
fter*, & they alfo ſhewed fad teſtimonies
of their forrow. This rumor did fly as
farre as *Argenis's* eares, who would not
furvive *Him*, having as *She* thought, loſt
Him, who made *Her* take all the delight
She had in the world. *Seleniſſa* brake this
defigne, by her wifedome, ſhewing unto
Her that *She* ought not fo flightly to
give faith to a rumor, who had no
affured Authour. That affwaged fomething *Her* griefe, but did not altogether
heale the fore. *Her* thoughts were then
toffed, with irkfome cares, which altred
by little and little the beauty of *Her*
face. Alfo *Meleander* being come to entertaine *Her*, with *His* affaires, though
She had refolved, to oppofe *Her* conftancy, to *Her* mif-fortunes, and to fup-
preffe *Her* forrowes, for feare, that *Her*
Love fhould be knowne, neverthelefle
when *He* began the difcourfe, of *Poliar-*
chus

chus His accident, and to tell *Her* how *He* had bin conftrained, to abandon *Him*, to *His* enemies rage, *She* could be no longer miftris of *Her* fenfes, but fell downe in a trance, at the recitall of this adventure. *Seleniffa* fmothered this accident, in the beft wife fhe could, and affured the *King*, that *She* had had fundry fuch fits lately, but that fhe believed, there was nothing to be feared, and that they were but little faintings, caufed with the difpleafure, which *she* had fuffered during *Licogenes* his warre; *Her Father* left *Her*, amongft *Her* Women, who, with the feverall remedies they gave *Her*, made *Her* come to *Herfelfe* againe. But *She* received a full cure, by the newes which were brought unto *Her*, few daies after of *Her Poliarchus*, by an intimate friend of *His*, named *Arfidas*. This trufty confident had learn'd by *Gelanore*, a domefticke fervant unto *Poliarchus*, the truth of *His* Hiftory, thereupon he came to finde *Him* out in *Timocleas* houfe, where having had conference (of all *His* affaires) with *Him*, *Poliarchus*

liarchus conjured him, to fee *His Faire Argenis*, in *His* name, and to know of *Her*, as of *His* Oracle, what *He* fhould doe, in this extremity; *He* knew to what end the rumor of *His* death had beene fpread; *He* had alfo had notice, with what violence the Commons (to fhew themfelves paffionate for the *Kings* fervice,) purfued *Poliarchus*, feeing, that being perfwaded, *He* was in *Timocleas* houfe, had runne thither, and without any refpect, had violently entred in't, to take and make *Him* prifoner. In which, having had no fucceffe, becaufe *Poliarchus* was in a place of fafety. They nevertheleffe, difcharged their choller, upon *His Fellow the Prince of Mauritania*, who was, at laft, conftrained, to fuffer *Himfelfe* to be led captive, unto *Meleander*, as if it had beene *He* whom they fought after. *Arfidas* then, who had feene all thefe violences, came to give *Argenis* notice of the ftate of *Her Poliarchus His* affaires. At thefe pleafing news *She* was as much troubled to keepe backe *Her* foule, and to hinder it, from

leaving

leaving the body, as *She* had beene, in
the exceſſe of *Her* griefe. But Joy ſetled
Her minde againe; inſomuch that the
rayes of this *Sunne* of the *Court*, began
to appeare againe. During which time,
newes were brought unto *Her*, that *Poliarchus* was led as a priſoner unto the
Court : But the intelligence, which *She*
had received, by *Arſidas* of *Archombrotus*
accident, hindred this ill rumor, from
making an impreſſion, upon *Her* ſpirit.
So that this cloud was ſoone over. As
the Commons, which had taken him,
were arrived at *Court*, one of the *Cap-
taines of the Guard*, ſeeing ſo faire a priſoner, in the hands of ruſticall men,
ask'd of him who conducted *Him*,
whàt that *Cavalleere* had done, whom
they us'd ſo rigorouſly. This *Head* of
the common people, having replyed,
that it was *Poliarchus*, whom the *King*
had commanded, ſhould be taken, that
He might be puniſh'd, according to juſtice; He began to ſmile, and ſaid unto
this people, that to ſpeake the truth,
they had ſhewed their fidelity, for the

Kings

Kings fervice, but that they had not fped, in this occafion, feeing their prifoner, was not *Poliarchus* which was fought for. Neverthelefle, *He* was led before *Meleander*, who, after *He* had praifed *His* fubjects zeale, addrefs'd *Himfelfe* unto *Arcombrotus*, and made *Him* a thoufand excufes, for this offence happened not by *His* command, but by the ignorance, of this people, who had miftaken themfelves, in *His* perfon. The *Prince of Mauritania*, though full of rage, to fee *Himfelfe* fo unworthily abufed, neverthelefle diflembled *His* choler, & making *His* complement, with a very comely behaviour, moft humbly defired *Him* to believe, that in what manner foever, *He* could bee brought before *Him*, *He* held it alwaies for a fingular glory, that *He* had the meanes, to offer *Him His* fervice. In fine, neverthelefle, fhewing *Himfelfe* more fenfible of the injury done to *His* friend, then to *Himfelfe*, *He* could not hinder *Himfelfe* from reprefenting his complaint, and faid with a haughty courage unto

Meleander.

Meleander. But, *concerning* Poliarchus
His *difgrace*, *which hath beene the fubject*
of my mif-fortune; Your Majefty, *will give*
me leave to tell Him, *that if accufations*
make crimes, there will bee no innocence,
affured in the world, fince, that the moft
juft, will by this meanes be expofed, unto
the rage of flander, which is perpetually,
about Princes *eares, to furprife and give*
them all manner of ill impreffions, againft
thofe which they would put out of favour.
Your Majefty *may be pleafed to remember*
Licogenes *his brazen face, and the info-*
lency, of all his confederates ? Doe not You
imagine alfo, that thofe who have made fuch
an outrage, againft the Crowne, *will fpare*
Your *beft* Servants? *Thofe who confpire*
againft Kings, *and that will have their*
Empires, *to grow defolate, doe firft endea-*
vour, to corrupt and feduce thofe whom
they know to bee moft paffionate for their
fervice, and when they cannot doe it, make
ufe of other crafts, to caufe their Mafters
to fufpect their fidelity, to the end that da-
ring not to truft them any more, they fhould
remaine wholly unufefull unto them, I have

D   *learn'd*

learn'd of a Lady *of this* Court (*who by chance was in company with that* Cavalleer, *when I firft faw* Him,) *the great affiftance which* He *hath given* You, *in the Warre, that thofe feditious have moft unhappily kindled in the middeft of* Your Kingdome, *and the hurt which* He *hath done to* Your *enemies.* The griefe *which they have conceived thereat hath caufed them, to feeke out the meanes to make* Him *away, by open violence, that they might rob* You *of that powerfull prop, of* Your *State.* But this *defigne having fayled, by the great valour that was in* Him *whom thefe cowards affaulted;* They *now have had recourfe unto vayled artificiall deceits.* And to *circumvent* Your *goodneffe, doe father upon an innocent, the odiouſneffe of an action, where there's no crime, but that which proceeds from their perfidiouſneffe.* Your Majefty *who hath purchas'd fo much glory, by the true execution of* Juftice, *not onely amongft* His *fubjects, but alfo amongft ftrangers, will referve, if* He *pleafes, an eare for* Poliarchus, *to learne by* His *owne mouth, the particulars of this encounter, which trou-*

bles

bles all Your Court, *and may be pleaſed to*
remember, *that though* He *were guilty*, *it*
would alwaies bee a kinde of injuſtice, *to*
condemne Him, *and not heare* His *reaſons.*
And if Your Majeſty *will grant*, *that I*
may finde out the truth of this buſineſſe by
thoſe meanes, *which are uſed amongſt* Cavalleers, *I offer my ſelfe to enter in com-*
bate againſt the authors of this ſlaunder. I
am ſure that having the Gods, (*whom they*
have offended,) *for their enemies*, *and that*
having a continuall remorſe, *in their conſci-*
ences, *their armes will fall from their hands*,
and that their cowardiſe will bee a viſible
proofe, *of the infamous treaſon*, *whereof they*
have beene the inventors. The *King*, who
was a generous *Prince*, was not offen-
ded at *Archombrotus* His freedome, but
by the mildneſſe of *His* face and ſpee-
ches, teſtified altogether the beliefe *He*
had of *Poliarchus His* innocence, and
the eſteeme *He* made of *His* friends
great courage, who offered *Himſelfe* ſo
freely to fight, in the behalf of *His* cauſe.
All the *Court* made acclamations of joy,
at this lofty teſtimony, which the *Prince*

of Mauritania rendred unto *Poliarchus,*
Argenis who tooke the beſt part therein, thank'd him, with much curteſie, and
by this civility, did put *Herſelfe* in danger to ſpoile all, ſeeing that *Archombro-*
tus who had nothing of the *Moore* but
the name, being kept backe, in *Her Fa-*
thers ſervice, and having gotten the reputation of the moſt valiant *Cavalleere*
in the world, after *Poliarchus,* was ſur-
priſed with vanity, which made *Him* ſo
farre to forget, all *His* promiſes, that *He*
became *His* friends Rivall, and endeavoured to rob *Him* of the *Princeſſe.* In the
meane time *Argenis,* ſends a diſpatch
by *Arſidas* to *Poliarchus,* conjures *Him*
by *Her* letters, to believe that all theſe
croſſes of fortune, were uſefull onely, to
encreaſe *Her* love, rather then to dimi-
niſh it, that *Argenis* will never be to any,
but to *Poliarchus,* that *She* paſſionatly
deſired *She* might aſſure *Him* thereof,
with *Her* owne mouth but that *She*
feares, leaſt comming to *Court He*
ſhould be knowen; therefore let *him*
take the ſureſt party, and if *He* thinkes

it

it fit, *He* should returne in *His Kingdome:*
But that *He* should not forget, to cause
His greatnesse to appeare, by bringing
so faire an army, from *His Countrey,* that
amongst the obstacles, which might
oppose themselves to *their* designe, *He*
should be able to free *Her* from those
cares and troubles, which *Their* separa-
tion causes, that in the meane time, *Shee*
will indeavor, to change *Her Fathers* anger and bring *Him* againe, in *His* favour.
Which *She* imagines will not be very
difficult, considering the esteeme which
He makes, of *His* vertue. *Poliarchus* having read this letter, could not tell
what to resolve. The imagination, of
the perill and feare to be discovered,
caus'd *Him* to apprehend the journey to
Court, where he doubted not, but *His* e-
nemies, were watching to surprise *Him.*
Arsidas and *Timoclea* fearing, least *He*
should miscarry, represented *Him* the
danger, yet greater then it was. But the
desire *He* had to see *Argenis,* made *Him*
despise all the hazzards, which they represented. *He* then calls aside, *His* deare

friend, and declares unto *Him*, that *He* had rather expose *Himselfe* to *His* enemies rage, then to goe out of *Sicily*, and not see the *Princesse*. *Arsidas* seeing the ardour of *His* passion, in lieu of opposing, fortifies it, by the assurance which he gives *Him*, to runne the same hazard. They take leave of *Timoclea*, unto whō *Poliarchus* protested, to be so much obliged, that it is out of *His* power, to acknowledge the innumerable courtesies, which she hath heap'd upon *Him*; conjures her to believe, that at least, she hath a *Crowne* and a *King* at her devotion; assures her, that *Hee* will returne into *Sicily*, so well accompanied, that the greatnesse of *His* birth, shall not bee doubted, and that then, *He* shall have some manner of meanes, to acknowledge the good offices, which *His* trusty friends have done him; and then addes, that *He* is going to make use, of the perriwigge, and beard (whereof she had made *Him* a present) to disguise *Himselfe*. Thus with an extreame sorrow *He* takes *His* leave of this vertuous *Lady*,

which

which did fhed, an Ocean of teares at
His departure *He* foone after arrived
at *Court*, with *Arfidas His* Conduct,
where immediately after, *He* gives notice unto *Argenis* of *His* coming, the joy
which *She* received thereat, cannot be
expreft; but feeing *Him*, with a forme,
fo different, from that of *Poliarchus, She*
did fhed fome teares, feeing in what
danger, *He* did precipitate *Himfelfe* for
Her fake: on the other fide, the contentment which *She* received, to fee before
Her eyes, that which *She* held moft
deare in the world, caufed *Her*, prefently to leave off *Her* teares. It was in
the *Temple*, in the middeft of the devotions and facrifices, where they faw each
other, but it was impoffible to continue
this practice, full of danger, any longer;
Argenis fent *Him* word by *Arfidas* that
Hee fhould with expedition faile into
France, to raife there, with promptitude,
an army able, not onely, to overcome
the *Kings* enemies, but alfo all *Sicily.*
Arfidas undertooke to fraight a fhip, for
that voyage, under colour that he had

another

another to make in *Jtaly*. They imbarque themſelves, intending to hold their courſe towards *France*, but the fates diſpoſed otherwiſe of it.

In the meane time, the Warre is kindled afreſh, and the *Confederates*, having reunited their forces, cauſed all the *State*, to rebell againſt the *King*, who had but foure *Holds* remayning, in one of which (being ſcituat in an Iſland) *He* retired *Himſelfe* with *Argenis*, and the choyce of his truſtieſt Servants. In this diſtreſſe, Fortune brought forth new cauſes of trouble, unto *Poliarchus* and the *Princeſſe*. The yong *King of Sardany and Corſe*, taken with *Argenis's* beauty, whereof the glory as well as the pictures had flowen, throughout all the Univerſe, makes a puiſſant Army, takes *His* courſe towards *Sicily*, and arrives with *His* Navy, neere unto the *Towne* where *Meleander* had retired *Himſelfe*. The ſight of ſo many Sayles, frights all the *Kings* party, as if they had beene new enemies, arrived to diſſipate the relickes of *His* fortune. But the *King of*

of Sardany, sends to *Meleander,* gives *Him*
assurance of *His* Army, and declares
Him, that taking that interest which *He*
ought, in the common case of *Kings, He*
was come to assist *Him,* and to helpe
Him to chastise *His* subjects rebellion.
This new joy, causes *Him* to open *His*
Gates, and the *King Himselfe* prepares to
goe, and receive *Him,* in *His* owne ship-
ping. But being desirous to take away
all suspition unto *Meleander,* and *His;*
He commands *His* Navy to remaine in
the roade, till they had newes of *Him,*
and with a small traine, goes to meete
with *Meleander,* who with a great freedome leapes into *His* Ship, to honour
Him so much the more. After the com-
plements, the *King of Sardany,* to witnesse, that *He* had no lesse confidence,
then that of *Sicily,* goes in *His* Gally, and
went in company together towards the
Towne, where *Meleander* receives *Him,*
with as much magnificence, as the state
of *His* affaires would permit. Having
courted a while, *He* hastens the warre,
and being enflamed with the love of
Argenis,

Argenis, whom *He* had found much fairer, then *Her* picture, wifhes for nought elfe, but Combats, defiring to make *Himfelfe* remarkeable in them, to fhew *Himfelfe* worthy of the love of fo faire a *Princeffe.* Archombrotus is jealous of this new Rivall, doth proteft in *His* heart, *He* will never yeeld *Him* this glory, which *He* could not fuffer that it fhould be enjoyed by another, which was better then *He,* who was *Poliarchus.* Thefe yong *Cavalleers,* edg'd on by their paffions, doe wonders againft the enemies. But the *Moore,* was fo happy, that having faved *Meleanders* life, *He,* with *His* owne hand, flew the chiefe of the factious; Neverthelefle, the forces which the *King of Sardany* had brought, which doubtlefle had opened the way unto the Victory, feemed exceeding confiderable unto the *King and Court of Sicily.* Being all returned in the place where *Faire Argenis* was, the onely fubject of fo many heroicall actions, jealoufie inflames it felfe; the *Moore,* (though covertly) imployes all his induftry, to
purchafe

chafe the *Princeſſes* favour, who hath *His* follicitations in difdaine, and detefts in *Her* heart, fo vifible an infidelity, which tends onely, to make a fhamefull wound in *Her* conftancy. *The King of Sardany* asketh *Her* in marriage openly unto *Her Father*, who dares not refufe *Her*, after fo powerfull a fuccour wherewith *He* hath newly oblig'd *Him*. Neverthelefle knowing that *His Daughter*, had no inclination, for that *Prince*, *He* makes ufe of all manner of artificiall delayes, to feede *Him* with vaine hopes, without breaking with *Him*, fearing leaft being moved with *His* refufall, *He* fhould turne *His* armes againft *Sicily*. But where art thou *Poliarchus* ?

Some few months before, *He* had fhipp'd himfelfe in that Veffell, which, *Arſidas* had caufed, to be prepar'd, to fayle towards the *Gaules :* but *He* was beaten, with fuch contrary winds, and *His* Ship was fo much perfecuted, with tempeftuous ftormes, that *He* was conftrain'd, to abandon it, and put *Himſelfe*, under the mercy of the waves in a little Cock-

Cock-boat, which went and fplit it felf, neere unto a rock, where, with much trouble *He* faved *Himfelfe*, with *His* trufty *Gelanore*: But it was not the end of *His* adventures. Perceaving from the top of this clift, a Brigantine which fay-led upon the fea, *He* began to call out, and to conjure, thofe which were with-in it, that they fhould take pitty at *His* misfortune: They were *Pyrates*, who had no feeling of humanity: Neverthe-leffe imagining that thofe who call'd them, had faved fome great riches, among'ft the relickes of their Ship-wrack, they came neere the Rock, and tooke them in their Brigantine. *Poliar-chus His* port, and the fumptuous cloathes, wherewith *He* and *Gelanore* were clad, was like to be their vndo-ing: The Captaine with his conforts, would have put them to the Chayne. *Poliarchus*, aftonifd at this barbarouf-neffe, retires a ftep backwards, and put-ting *His* hand upon *His* fword, askes *Him* whence came this change, having newly faved *His* life? Defires him, not

to

to blot so great an obligation, by so
bloody an outrage. But *He* speakes to a
barbarous man, to whom intreaties en-
venom and swell the courage. *Poliarchus*
who would dispute *His* liberty, takes
hold on a peece of an oare, whereof
He makes use in lieu of a buckler, and
drawing *His* sword, shewes that *He* is
not a man, to suffer that affront; *Gelanore* seconds *Him*: They fight, but the
match was so vnequall, that the *Prince*
had infallibly bin lost, if some prisoners
(unto whom *He* had the dexterity to
cut their bonds wherewith they were
tyed, arming themselves, with the Pyrates owne armes, which they had
slayne) had not succor'd them. At last
this assistance made *Him* victorious, and
master of the Brigantine, and fortune of
those which were within it. *He* learn't
by the Galli-slaves, and prisoners, that
those Pyrates, had newly taken a great
prey, in *Mauritania*, and that they had
carried away, all the *Queenes* Treasure,
who had an vncomfortable sorrow
thereof. One of them, to whom *Poliar-*

chus

chus had faved the life, told *Him* all the particulars thereof, and alfo fhewed *Him*, the place where the Boxes were hidden. *Poliarchus* having caufed them all to be opened; was aftonied, at the fight of fo much riches, together, and then thought it fit, that being fo neere unto the *Queenes* Territories, *He* was, (in Honor) obliged, to feeke *Her* out, and to reftore unto *Her Her* Treafure, to free *Her* from the affliction wherein this loffe had plunged *Her*. But as they were throwing the dead over-boord, *He* perceaved, that *His* folkes were fearching one, upon the fands, of whom having pulled off one of his buskins; they found a packet of letters very carefully bound up upon his legge. Curiofity, made *Him* defire to fee what it was; *He* perceaves prefently, that the letters were directed unto *Him*, and having opened them, fees the name of *Licogenes*, which was he who writ unto *Him*. The little love they bare one to another made *Him* admire this novelty: But having read them exactly, *He* was ftrucke

with

with an incomparable aſtoniſhment, greater then the firſt, wherein *He* had found *Himſelfe*.

Licogenes having had notice that *Argenis* had made *Poliarchus His* peace with *Meleander*; and that *Meleander*, to aſſure *Him* of *His* good will, did not onely write unto *Him*, but alſo ſent *Him* a rich Bracelet, in token of *His* affection; had found the meanes, to cauſe this preſent, to be poiſon'd, by the artificiall cunning of one of his confidents; and to cauſe the horror of his crime to fall on *Meleander*, had ſent him who was found amongſt the dead in this ſhip, to the end he might give notice unto *Poliarchus*, of the treaſon, which was intended towards *Him*.

Poliarchus having ſeene by *Licogenes His* letters, the advice which *He* gave *Him*, could never imagine that *He* had ſo much care of *His* life, nor that a great *King* would have procured *Him* ſuch an infamous death. *He* puts off the deliberation of the buſineſſe; till *Hee* was arrived in *Mauritania*, where at the in-

ſtant

ftant he caufed the Brigantine to faile;
He fent *His Gelanore* before, to advertife
the Queene of *His* arrivall, and to affure *Her* that *He* brought backe *Her*
Treafure which *He* had taken from the
hands of the Pyrates. Thefe newes re-
joyc'd the *Affrieans*, but the *Queene* could
not imagine that *Her* Treafure was yet
whole; and there was fomething in it,
when it was taken, which troubled *Her*
more then all the reft. *She* takes what
was next to *Her*, and goes to the Sea-
fhore, to welcome *Poliarchus*. At their
meeting, *He* falutes *Her*, and declares
unto *Her* that *He* believes that Heaven
had conducted *Him* by this tempeft
about this coaft, to quench *Her* teares,
fince *He* brought *Her* backe all *Her* riches, which *She* had fo much deplor'd.
The Queene impatient to know the
truth, leaps aboard, where *He* followes
and fhewes *Her* immediately the Boxes,
well lock'd up. *She* opens them, and
found therein all what *She* fought for,
and particularly the Cabinet, which
ferv'd afterwards to reconciliate *Her*

Sonne with *Poliarchus*. Then *She* cryed out with great joy, and imbracing the *Prince*, called *Him*, the *God Saviour of Mauritania*, thence *She* led him to *Her Palace*, and forgot no kinde of magnificence and good entertainement, to testifie how welcome *He* was. Amongst all this mirth and gladnesse *Poliarchus His* soule was all troubled with *Licogenes His* letters, & though *He* could not suspect *Meleander* of this perfidiousnesse, *He* was not fully satisfied of *Him*; To pull out all these thorns from *His* soule, *He* resolves to send *Gelanore* into *Sicily*, and to give him letters to *His Argenis*, but not unto *Meleander*, to whom *He* was contented to send *Licogenes His* letters, to the end *Gelanore* might judge by *His* countenance what *He* had in *His* soule, and if one might believe of *Him* so unworthy a wickednesse. It was in a good time that *Gelanore* arrived in *Sicily*, because *Arsidas* accompanied with *Timonides*, which was he unto whom *Meleander* had given the Bracelet to carry, was going to spread abroad the rumour

E   of

of *Poliarchus His* death throughout
all the *Court*.　The *Pilote* of the ship in
which *He* had made shipwracke, having
by good fortune saved himselfe, had
brought word unto *Arsidas* of the misfortune which was happened unto *Him*,
and had described unto him the manner of *His* losse.　*Arsidas* having at the
same time met with *Timonides*, and
learn'd of him the subject of his journey, had stayed it, and had made him
partaker of these bad newes.　They
had then gone together very sad unto
the *Court*, knowing not how to publish
this accident, which was enough to
cause *Argenis's* death with sorrow. The
first whom they encountred at their
landing was *Gelanore* which came from
Affricke from the *Prince of France* : At
the sight of him they thought they had
beene in another world, because they
had bin assured he had perish't with his
Master: it was then as a sunne of good
hope which began to shine upon them.
But said they unto him; *Gelanore*, where
is *Poliarchus*? the ill newes which wee
                                    have

have heard puts us in such trouble, that wee cannot beginne our complement, but with this question. *Poliarchus* is very well, replied *Gelanore*; I have left *Him* in *Affrick*, and am come to see the *Princesse* on *His* behalfe. You revive us, replied the *Princes* two friends, without any further delay *Argenis* must have notice of it, for feare least this ill rumor which wee have heard should have bin spread in the *Court*, *Arsidas* vndertakes this commission, and assoone receaves a command to fetch *Gelanore*. When he comes before the *Princesse*, he kisses the letters, and presents them unto *Her* together with his *Masters* commendations: *She* tooke a singular content at the reading of the letters : But when *She*, had opened *Licogenes His* letter, *She* was seized with horror, and resolv'd that *Her Father* should see them, as also *Gelanore* had order to present them unto *Him*. *Meleander* having seene them conceav'd an extraordinary spite, not only against *Licogenes*, but also against *Poliarchus*, that without writing, had sent unto

E 3 *Him,*

Him, such infamous letters, of a traitor;
and testified not unto *Him* the little
faith which *He* gave to them. Insomuch
that as *Gelanore* who had all the *Princesses* dispatches, went to take leave of
Him, and ask't *Him* if he would not do
the honor unto *His Master* to write to
Him. Go your wayes, said he, *and tell your
Master, that I am a King , and not a Poiso-
ner:* Neverthelesse that caused two of
Licogenes's friends, who had lately bin
arrested, to be tortur'd, as having plotted something against the *Kings* honor,
and against the quiet of *His State, Gelanore* went backe, towards *Mauritania,*
where he found *Poliarchus* yet sicke of
His fever. Having delivered *Him* the
Princesses letters; he told *Him* all the
particulars of the *Court of Sicily,* and a-
mongst other things, complained, of *Archombrotus His* great pride, who would
not daigne to looke upon him, insinua-
ting thereby , openly enough, that he
beleeved he aspir'd to marry the *Princesse;*there needed no more to put*Poliarchus* in the field. Then, notwithstanding
Gelanores

Gelanore's remonftrances who charg'd
Him on the behalfe of *Argenis*, to go in
His Kingdome and bring fuccours, to put
Sicily in liberty, *He* refolv'd to returne,
difguif'd as before, in *Meleanders Court*;
And to that end, feekes out the cure of
His ague, in a ftrange remedy, having
better fucceeded therein, then the *Phy-
fitians* had judged;he went prefently to
take *His* leave of the *Queene*, who
would by all meanes ftay him : but *He*
alleag'd *Her* fo many reafons, that *she*
was forc't to let *Him* go, for feare *she*
fhould be a hindrance in the effecting of
the great affaires which (as *He* faid) *He*
had in hand. *she* would have given *Him*
magnificent prefents, but *He* who
would not take any thing, of all *Her*
treafures, but one only ring, which perforce *She* caufed *Him* to accept,remai-
ned fatiffied with the honor of *Her* favour,and having fhip't *Himfelfe*, haftned
fo much the Pilote and Mariners,that in
a fhort time *He* arriv'd at the *Court of Sicily*. *Gelanore* had charge to advertife
Arfidas, to the end he fhould beare the

E 3 newes

newes unto the *Princesse*; he did it with
such dexterity, that there is *Poliarchus*
amongst the *King of Sardany's* and *Archombrotus His* practises, neere unto *His
Argenis,* under favour of *His* borrowed
face. The joy which *They* received at
the sight of each other, is beyond ex-
pression : The conclusion of *Their* enterview was, that at this present *He*
should breake all obstacles, and should
goe directly in *His Kingdome,* to leavie
a puissant Army, that *He* might free *Her*
out of the hands of so many Suters, who
were so importunate unto *Her. He* then
leaves *Sicily,* and happily arrives in *His
Realme, where He raises* a Royall Army,
which *He* presently ships, for the effecting of this great voyage, and to shew
unto the eyes of *Sicily,* as a sparkling of
the glory of *His* birth. But it happened,
that being at Sea, the Navy was beaten with a furious storme, that intending to hold their course towards *Sicily, He* was cast upon the Coast of *Mauritania,* where *He* found wherewith to
cause *His* valour to appeare, and to give
that successe to *His* affaires, which *He*

did not imagine, should be there. Neverthelesse *His* absence, a hundred times
blam'd by *Argenis*, which could not tell
what Starre to accuse, of this misfortune, was the cause that the *Moore* and
the King of Sardany continued their pursuits; The *Sardiot* imagining *He* was
abus'd, resolved to steale away *Argenis*,
and to ship *Her* in *His* owne Navy, and
so returne with so rich a Prey into *His*
Kingdomes. The *Moore*, who had an
eye on all sides, discovers this designe,
advertises the *King*, and gives *Him* such
true tokens thereof, that *Meleander* gives
notice unto *Radiroboranes* that *He* igno-
red not *His* practices, which gave *Him*
cause to breake wholly with *Him*. To
be reveng'd on *Meleander*, *He* writ *Him*
a letter, full of contempt and outrages
against *Argenis*, whose Governesse *He*
had suborned, which had discovered
unto *Him*, *Poliarchus His* secrets and
Their loves, *Meleander* afflicted beyond
measure of this affront, is angry with
Argenis, which justifies *Her* innocence, by
she her selfe who had betrayed *Her*. This

E 4　　　　　mise-

miferable wretch feeing her felfe difcovered did feeke (by the meanes of
poifon) the expiation of her crime, and
procur'd her owne death, before the
eyes of the *Court*. *Meleander* to fhun a
greater mif-fortune, and to fortifie
Himfelfe with friends, went to *His Daughter*, & fpeakes to Her to marry the *Prince
of Mauritania*, of whofe merit and valour
He fpake advantagioufly to enduce *Her*
to confent. *She* demands fome time to
refolve *Herfelfe*, and reprefents unto
Him, that it would bee a fhame for a
Kings Daughter, to give *Her* faith fo
flightly unto a man who had not fo
much as demanded it, with the folem-
nities accuftomed in like occurrences.
Her Father grants *Her* two months time,
and Fortune lengthned this terme :
The King of Sardany full of rage and de-
fpight, for fo bloody an affront, puts
under fayle, leaves *Sicily*, and having a
favourable wind, within a fhort time,
arrives in *His Kingdome*. *His* foule being
wounded, caufes *Him* to undertake revenge (of the injury which *He* had received

ceived in the *Court of Sicily*) upon *Mauritania* ; *He* imagined that *He* could
eaſily conquer that Great *Kingdome*,
where there was but a *Queene*, which
held the reines of the *Empire* ; but the
ſtorme, which was like to caſt away *Poliarchus*, ſaved the *Moores* and their
Crowne. The tempeſt having caſt *Him*
upon that coaſt, *He* offers *His* Army,
unto their *Queene*, who knew the obligation which *She* had unto *Him* in the
formervoyage : *She* accepted thoſe ad-
vantageous offers, and recommended
unto *Him*, the ſafety of *Her State*. After
many encounters, ſometimes the victory
was ſeene to leane on the *Sardinians*
ſide, and ſometimes on the *Affricans*,
aſſiſted with the *Gaulois*. At laſt they
came to a ſet battell, which having been
bloody amongſt the ſouldiers, was no
leſſe cruell betwixt the *Generals*. Theſe
two generous *Princes* edg'd on, by a
ſecret hatred which they bare one to
another, ſorted themſelves during the
horror of the fight, and filled with a
furious animoſity, cauſed their ſouldiers

diers to retire, that they might end the
Combat, and end their differences by
the death of the one or the other ; After
a great conflict they were separated
twice : But both aspiring to the victory,
and being impatient at this succour, out
of rage and despite threatned their
souldiers to fall on them, if they had
the audacity to hinder them any more.
They beginne their conflict the third
time, but they appeared so wearied and
weakned by reason of the losse of their
blood, that it was thought the Conquerour should have no great cause to glo-
rifie himselfe of his victory, at the end
of the Combat.   In the end neverthelesse *Poliarchus* who had some advan-
tage upon the *Sardiot*, for the last blow,
finding out a place through the defect
of *His* Armour, thrusts *His* sword
through *His* throat, and sacrifices *Him*
to the *Princesse of Sicily's* wrath; *Radiro-*
branes whose soule was already upon *His*
lips thrust *Himselfe* on *Poliarchus*, and
fell downe upon *Him* : but being be-
reaved of life, *Poliarchus* disingag'd
Him-

Himfelfe by little and little, from under this body, and appeared victorious in the *Head* of *His* Troopes: The *Moores* know not what Trophies to erect, to the *French Princes* vertue; their *Queene* avouches, that *Her Sonne* and *She* owe unto *His* courage, all the remainder of the good fortune which they have in the world. Going to visit *Him*, when *He* was sicke, of the wounds which *He* had received in the Combat, after many praises said to the Conquerours glory, *She* speaks unto *Him* of the happy purchase, which *Her Sonne* had made in *Sicily*, and in few words gives *Him* to understand that *Meleander*, holding *Himfelfe* extreamely obliged unto *His* valour, had offered *Him His Daughter* in marriage. At this word all *Poliarchus His* wounds did bleed afresh, and feemes by the palenesse of *His* face, that *His* foule is going to abandon *His* body, as being weary to dwell in it : But this is not all, here's a mightier wave, which comes to encounter *Him*, to banish out all patience from *His* foule. The *Queene* had

had conjurd *Her* Sonne by *Her* letters, that *He* fhould make a journey into *His Kingdome*, before *He* married the *Prin-ceffe of Sicily*, and to induce *Him* to make this voyage, had reprefented unto *Him* the mif-fortunes whereof *His State* was threatned by the *K. of Sardany's* Army. Ther *He* is come, and led to *Poliarchus His* chamber, whō *He* had cruelly offen-ded: *Poliarchus* feared not this encounter at all, becaufe the *Moore* bore another name in *Sicily*, then in *His Kingdome*, but knowing *His* Rival, remēbers what the *Queene* had told *Him*, touching *Her Sons* marriage with *Argenis*. Griefe fo over-maftered *His* fenfes, that at this fight, all full of rage, he turn'd *His* head on the other fide, fhews tokens of *His* fpight, and receaves no better countenance of the *Moore*; who refolves to avenge *Him-felfe* of the obftacle, which *He* gives to *His* Nuptials, imagining, that the delay, w^ch *Argenis* had ask't, was for *His* fake: They come to words which teftifie the great adverfionwhich they have againft each other. The *Queene* much aftonied,

brings

brings forth *Her Son* out of the sick mans chamber, chides *Him* for *His* incivility, represents unto *Him* the obligation w^ch *He* hath to the *French Prince*, and by way of reproach, gives *Him* to understand, that *He* shall be for ever blamed, to have so unworthily used an outlandish *Prince*, unto who *His Crown* is so strictly oblig'd. In the meane time examining exactly the cause of so cruell a hatred, who had made *Poliarchus*, to resolve to take Sea, thus sicke and ill as *He* was, *She* finds out, that it was Iealousie, which they had each of the other concerning *Argenis*, which had stirred up this storme: That comforts *Her*, beleeving *She* had found the meanes to agree them without much trouble. *She* speakes to both the *Princes*; Imperiously, to *Her Sonne*; Courteously, unto that of *France* : *She* conjure *Them*, to referre the decision of their differences, unto *Meleander*: *And I will cause*, (said *She* unto *Poliarchus*) *that you shall have the* Faire Argenis, *and that my* Son *shall not loose* Her This promise, as an Oracle, with two faces, doth

astonish

aftonifh the *Princes*, but the refpect
which they bare to the *Queene*, obliges
them to beleeve *Her*, and to give a true
Faith, unto *Her* words, and ftay with
patience, what the event will be, whereof both the one and the other feemed
to hope well. Thus, *Poliarchus* is conjured to remaine in the *Court of Mauritania* to caufe *His* wounds to be healed,
and in the meane time the *Moore* lands
His Navy in Sardany full of factions by
the death of their *King*. *He* conquers it
with little trouble; *He* comes backe
Victorious to meet the *Queene his Mother*, which at *Poliarchus His* intreaty,
difpatches them both with *Her* letters,
to goe, and decide their difference,
before *Meleander* unto whom they had
referred it by *Her* Counfell. *She* gives
a *Cabinet*, unto *Her fonne*, to carry unto
Meleander; the pretious ftones which
were in it, were of an ineftimable value,
but that was not the fecret. Having
taken leave of the *Queene*, the two *Rivall Princes*, hoife up faile, fhewing no
figne of anger, againft each other: They
                    arrived

arrived much about one time in *Melean-*
ders Court. *Argenis* hath notice that *Po-*
liarchus is fo neere unto her: This joy
had tranfported *Her*, ifrage had not
crofft it, when *She* heard, that *He* had
made *Her Father* Umpire of *Her* marriage.*Is it then,* faid *She,* *all the efteeme* He
makes of me, to put Himfelfe thus in hazard,
to lofe Me? And if my Father *who hath an*
inclination for the Moore, *gives* Me *unto*
Him, *doth he thinke, that I will ever con-*
fent thereunto *? Before that fhall happen,*
fteele,or poifon fhall put Me *out of the world:*
I fhall have more courage then He*: my death*
fhall blot out all the Trophies that this
Moore *goes fancying in his minde, and*
Poliarchus *fhall know that I can love,more*
conftantly, and truly then He.*At leaft if* My
fexe takes away the meanes , to difpute
againft Him, *the glory of Armes, nothing*
fhall hinder Me , *to take from* Him *that of*
Conftancy. *This lift is open to all the coura-*
gious fpirits, without diftinction of fexe,
and I fhall not be the firft Virgin, who hath
furpaffed men, in fidelity.

In the meane time the two *Lovers* are
favourably

favourably receaved at *Court*, where *Poliarchus* began to reaffume *His* lufter, and as it were, to darken a little the *Prince of Mauritanias* glory, they go to falute the *King*, who at firft fight, makes them the beft welcome which they can defire. *Poliarchus* was the firft which made *His* complement in few words. But the *Moore* having prefented thofe letters with the *Cabinet* whereof *His Mother* had charged *Him* to give unto *Meleander*, faw *Himfelfe* ingaged in a longer difcourfe.

At the opening of the letters, the *King* changed colour, having read them very exactly, and with an extraordinary attention, *He* tooke a little Golden Key, which the *Queene of Mauritania* had inclofed in them, and opened the *Cabinet*, where *He* found things, which did ballance *His* Spirits in fuch fort, that among'ft the tokens, which *He* gave of *His* contentment, the teares were feene to trickle downe *His* cheekes, in fuch abundance, that all the company was aftonied thereat. At the inftant forgetting

ting *Himselfe* a little in point of ciuility,
He left the *Prince of France* alone, and
drew the *Moore* aside as to entertaine
Him more privatly and with more
liberty ; this negligence was nothing to what followed : holding of
Him aside, takes *Him* about the necke,
imbraces and kisses *Him*, and gives *Him*,
the most sensible testimonies which *He*
could wish, of *His* affection. Not contented with that, *He* sent in all hast for
His Daughter, to whom as *She* arrived,
He said softly, some few words accompanied with an action which seemed to
be an image of joy, in *His* heart. The
Princesse taking no heed to what was so
neere unto *Her*, advances to salute the
Moore with visible signes of Love, *Poli-*
archus remaines astonied at this spectacle, and knowes not how to behave
Himselfe, but judging by the good entertainment, which *Argenis* gave unto
Archombrotus, that all his hopes were
ruinated, and that *His* rivall was going
to triumph, with *His* pursuits ; yielded
unto despaire, and in the bitternes of *His*

thoughts,

thoughts, began to say within *His* soule; *Is this then the fruit of so many paines which I have taken , and so many hazards which I have runn'd, to assure* My selfe *of the love, of this prodigious inconstancy,* She *to whom the most violent rigors of a* Father *, with a thousand Martyrdomes ought not to have chang'd , nor altered , suffers* Herselfe *to be surpris'd by some flatteries, which this* Old man *rounds* Her *in the eare:What mountaines of gold ? What perpetuall springs of felicity , have beene promissed* Her *, thus to change* Her *affection, and alter* Her *minde? unfortunate* Queene of Mauritaniá, *a scion of the old stock , what characters and inchantments hast thou made, upon those letters, to print upon them, that force , and give them that power, to cause so monstruous a change, and to ruinate in so small a time , that which* I *had built with so long a patience? How am* I *punished of the folly which* I *have committed, trusting in the words of a* Woman *and unto the promisses of a* Damzell, *whereof the cunning and lightnesse, (qualities unseparable to that sexe) ought to have made me to suspect*

                       them

them more then the Winds which have brought and driven me on this infamous Shore: But however, If Poliarchus *hath beene deceaved,* He *can take such a cruel vengeance, that neither the Authors, nor confederates of this perfidiousnesse shall have no great cause to build triumphs, nor erect trophies to their vanity.* This wretched Old man, *who by the artificiall deceits whereof* He *is full, hath alwayes opposed my contentments, and these two insolent Lovers, who sport at the ship-wracke of my fortune, shall be the sacrifices of* My fury: *But it is not all,* I will also dye, *to the end my* Ghost *may pursue and persecute that ungratefull* Argenis, *unto the Throne of the immortall* Gods: *Before whom I will reproach* Her *prodigious infidelity, that a thousand oathes taken in their name, ought to have stayed, if* She *had had the feeling and beliefe which* She *should have had of their power and justice;* It is apparent, that it was Poliarchus His good Genius, *or the* Tutelary Angell of Sicily, which busied His Spirit, in these Tragick thoughts, to stay His designe, and to divert Him during as much space as
needed,

needed, to give *Meleander* and *Argenis*, time to remember themselves, and to come and make their excuses. As *He* was then, upon the point to goe and execute so furious a designe, and to put *Meleander*, *Argenis*, and *His Rivall* out of the world, and after this bloody execution, to run *His* sword through *His* body, and by that meanes to leave Tragick tokens of *His* jealousie and despite: Those who seemed, to have too much neglected *Him*, came to themselves againe, and perceaving their fault, went towards *Him* to make their excuses, and discover the cause of this joy, which having ravish't them, out of themselves, had made them, to forget all civility: *Poliarchus* finds the charmes of *His* fury and frensie in their discourses and reasons: The *Moore* is acknowledged to be *Argenis's Brother*; the *Queene of Mauritania*, had discovered the *History* by *Her* letters, and had given such good tokens unto *Meleander*, that *He* could not doubt, but that *He* was *His Sonne*, and the true *Heire* of the two *Crowns*, insomuch

somuch that *Archombrotus* receiving the succession of *His Estates*, left freely the possession of the *Princesse His sister*, unto *Poliarchus*, who would not have changed it with a thousand *Scepters*.

Meleander, seing that the most part of the assistants, vnderstood nothing in these wonders, and that every one desired, a more particular enlightning, tooke the word, and making a short discourse of the voyage which *He* had made in *Affricke* during the heat of *His* youth, avowed that *He* had beene enamoured of a Beauty, whose favour having purchas't, *He* had at last married *Her* secretly, and that *His* affaires, having called *Him* backe into *Sicily*, *He* had left *Her* with child, of a *Sonne*, which was *Archombrotus*, whom, since *Hyanisbe*, seeing *Herselfe* without children, by the *King Her husband*, had supposed; fayning to have beene brought a bed of *Him*, that *She* had beene induc't thereunto, because *Her* Sister, (which was *She*, whom *He* had loved,) seing *Herselfe* ready to dye, in childe-
bed,

bed, had difcovered the Secret, unto *Her.* Therefore it was not to be doubted but that *Archombrotus* was *Argenis's Brother*, to whofe marriage for that caufe *He* could not afpire, but left the free poffeffion of her, unto *Poliarchus*, an Incomparable *Prince*, and worthy the Alliance of the greateft *Princeffe* of the earth; and accordingly, if ever *Sicily* had feene *Her felfe* at the height of good Fortune, it was now where the deftinies had brought it unto, by un-knowne meanes unto men, that there-fore all the World fhould give fignes of a publike gladneffe, and that every one fhould runne unto the *Temples* of their *Gods*, to give them a thoufand thankes, for fo many bleffings fhow-red downe upon *His Crowne.* At thefe words the people was feene tranfpor-ted with a fecret ravifhment, by gi-ving fuch teftimonies of joy, amongft their Feafts, and Sacrifices: *Meleander* with *Archombrotus* confent, offers the *Kingdome of Sardany*, unto *Poliarchus* for *Argenis's* Marriage; *Poliarchus* being marvellous

marvellous well contented ; makes ouverture of an Alliance , for *Archombrotus* with a *Sister* of *His*, D ughter *of France*, which doth accept this glorious party with a thousand thankes, so that the two *Crownes* of *France* and *Sicily* remained united with such strong Bonds, that it seemed , the destinies would make this Alliance, perpetuall.

On the other side , *Poliarchus* sees *Himselfe* at the height of *His* desires,seeing that *He* was in possession of *Her*, whom *He* loved more dearely, then *His* owne life. Truely even as the rigours of a long Winter, causes the Spring to be found more pleasing, so all the crosses which *He* had suffered in this pursuit, caused *Him* to finde the enjoying of it, so much the sweeter.

F I N I S.

The selection from *Ioannis Barclaii Argenis* (1622, *STC* 1390) is reproduced, by permission, from the Folger Shakespeare Library copy (shelfmark *STC* 1390), with title page substituted, by permission from the Newberry Library copy (shelfmark Case Y682 B226). The text block of the original measures 140 × 83 mm. Page 651 is misnumbered as 655.

Readings where the copy is blotted:

635.14	tantâ varietate
635.19	O sœcundum, ait,
635.23	preciosius debeat
635.25	tormenta, erumpens
635.26	hæc decora
635.27	irasci, O
635.28	utroque præ-
635.29	quòd sen-
635.30	Argenidum; u-
640.6	arte aliquâ
640.8	est anxiâ
640.11	hostibus nostri
640.12	Nec vos
640.17	in assur-
640.18	Quem cur
640.32	omnia ge-
642.16	in nos ruen-
642.18	Prægnan-
642.20	Supponi
642.22	commondum fœ-
642.24	fascini me-
642.30	ad nuptias
642.32	virtutes
648.22	fœdera dextras
649.1	tandem nubila rerum
649.2	En leniùs aura
649.3	sua dona favore
649.6	delubrum victimæ
649.8	aut pæane
649.8	erat, quæ
649.9	Timocleæ honos,
649.12	tutelísque præci-
649.13	præferebantur,
649.15	dieíque læticia
649.16	Si fas est
649.17	me marito
649.28	inter vere-
649.29	tenentum, monuerat
649.30	solicitaret

IOANNIS
BARCLAII
ARGENIS.

Secunda Editio.

SVMMA FIDE ET CVRA
concinnata, & perutilis Indicis ac-
cessione priori locupletior.

L O N D I N I,
Pro Societate *Bibliopolarum*
M.DC.XXII.

sent indolem illam nisi Regibus à diis non tribui.
Cùm verò & ipse Archombrotus euasit in equum,
vix formâ deterior, aut fortunam minori spiritu im-
plens, amictúque insignis quem Mauri regium ha-
bebant, incerta ac propè diuisa aliquandiu studia
fuere; moxque votis meliori præsagio confusis, v-
trique mirabili consensu applausum est.

Ibant ergo, tanquam rixarum immemores, suis
& Siculis Proceribus medij, longâ militum, longi-
orique populi turbâ, viam præeunte atque clauden-
te. Quicquid à portu ad vrbem itineris erat, intu-
entium & comitantium series vno examine obte-
xit. In vrbe matronæ virginésque fenestras impleue-
rant, mistis pueris, quibus ad spectaculi tâti memori-
â, animos aut subito metu, aut læticiâ pulsabant. Hu-
maniffimi Reges, memorésque qui eos sic colerent
haud esse suos ciues, non deerant salutando, non
oculos atque manus ferendo ad populum; donec
in regiæ vestibulo Meleander apparuit. Hunc
ad se pedibus properantem vbi simul conspexere,
de equis desilierunt. Excusantem deinde quòd
non præstò ad portum fuisset; neque verò id se de-
disse superbiæ, sed eorum legatis qui quò progre-
deretur præscripserant; ambo leniffimâ oratione
vetant in iuuenes, & iam olim hospites, superfluo
cultu esse. Gratulatus deinde Poliarcho victoriam,
& Archombroto Sardiniam, perplexè querebatur;
quòd olim passus esset tantæ Galliæ Rex priuatæ se
sortis in Siciliâ haberi.

Iam ad aulam peruenerant; inuitabátque hospites Meleander ad Solia, quibus excepti colloque-
rentur. Sed illi tunc rati aduenisse gerendæ rei tem-

pus, suſtinuere ambo gradum; porrigéuſque Meleandro Archombrotus literas matris, poſtulauit vt
eas extemplo perlegeret. Priùs enim acquieſcere ſe
non poſſe. Idem & Poliarchus rogauit. Rex mira-
tus quid hæ literæ haberent tam celeriter procuran-
dum, gemmam ſoluit, & prolixas exorſus eſt. Neque mora, Poliarchi & Archombroti, anxios vultus, haud paruæ perturbationis notæ percurrere
cœperunt. Quippe illos codicillos vterque tanquam propria fata ſpectabat. Si ſeciùs quàm pro-
miſerat Hyaniſbe res ceſſiſſet, ſi aut nulla fœdera,
aut ingrata offerrentur, iam comparabant ſe ad iur-
gium; iam arma, iam furorem animis præcipiebant.
Arculam quoque (ita mater iuſſerat) Archombrotus Meleandro ſimul cum literis obtulerat; quàm o-
lim Poliarchus vindicauerat à peiratis. Neque mul-
tum ex epiſtolâ Meleander legerat, cum attonitu
inſtar nunc ſeipſum cœpit affari, nunc in Archombrotum mittere oculos, repetere deinde epiſtolam,
morarſque in omnibus. Puſilla erat clauis incluſa
literis: ea ſcilicet quâ reſerari arculam oportebat.
Eam Rex auidè manu tenens, perſeuerabat in lecti-
one Epiſtolæ. Nihil amplius Poliarchus vel Archombrotus dubitabant quin aliquid magni ef-
ficaciſſimæ literæ afferrent. Tandem ad menſam
vicino parieti applicitam Meleander accedit, ſo-
lùſque curioſe in apertâ ciſtulâ recognoſcit quid
lateret. Aliquot epiſtolæ inerant; quas ille per-
lectas cum ſuſpiriis & fletu oſculabatur. Anu-
lus quoque, & arcanæ rei pignora quædam ip-
ſi notiſſima, fidem ſeni faciebant, vera ſcripſiſſe Hy-
aniſbem.

Ergo

Ergo victus magnitudine improvisi affectûs; simul à Poliarcho petit, ut excuset necessaria quædam arcana breviter exequentem, simul mirantem Archombrotum rapit familiariùs ad eandem illam mensam, & oculis literas Hyanisbes obijcit, quas ille dum legit, Meleander in ejus collum effunditur; móxque juvenis objectus ad genua, confusione oris, alióque quàm solebat venerationis genere, omnium qui astabant mentes permovit. Præcipuè Poliarchum scena illa turbabat. Viderétne æmulum suum, ad amplexus, & omnia intimæ charitatis indicia acciri? Staret ipse interim neglectus Meleandro, relictúsque scilicet qui colloqueretur Eurymedi? Is enim officij causâ paulatim ad illius latus accesserat, dùm Archombroto Meleander loquitur; ne indecenter in mediâ aulâ solus ille Rex esset. Hæc tumidè agitanti ingens ad sævissimam indignationem pondus accessit. Nam admonita Argenis à patre se vocari, intrat cœnaculum; cúmque Rex aliqua venientem docuisset quæ percipi à remotis non poterant, sponte ipsa cervicem Archombroti petentis osculum utraque manu junxit. Miscuère deinde lachrymas quas gaudio esse expressas ex reliquo vultu scires; dextrámque tanquam in fidissimi amoris sacramentum, in cupientis Archombroti manum inseruit.

Iam vicerat furor Poliarchi patientiam, erátque impetus hæc invisa sibi gaudia turbandi. Ignarus quos pejùs devoveret, Hyanisbem, Meleandrum, Archombrotum; adhuc aliquid ampliùs irascebatur, eminente rabie in Argenidem, quam ulcisci saltem illatâ sibi morte decreverat. Et ut omni sermo-

mone celerior est cogitatio, præsertim irata, multa
ille atque atrocia brevissimo tempore animo suo
complexus est. Hanc igitur mihi gratiam retulit Hyanisbe, per mea meorúmque vulnera incolumis?
Patebam incautus venenis; Ejus medicos adhibe-
bam ægritudini meæ; Sed noluit me perire, nisi
antè contemptus, & coràm violatus, non abjudica-
tam modò, sed fascinatam Argenidē in sui filij col-
lo aspicerem. Misisti me ad istius mortis atrocitatē,
venefica? Hæ sunt literæ, hæc promissa, hæc con-
cepta in penatum deorum auribus sacramēta? Sto-
lidiorem me, qui fidem expectabam in Africâ. Sed
non inulta fefelleris. Contraham tecum certamina,
contraham herculè ad internecionem tuæ gentis.
Quid cogito amens? & longorum solatiorum spē
tanquam victurus, solicito? Nónne vides quos perire illicò, sed tecum oporteat? Ibò; & carnifici
illi adimam spiritum, qui per meam victoriam Sardiniæ regno potitus, etiam hymenæum occupare
non dubitat; & ipverecundæ Argenidi saltem ejus
sanguine ruborem faciam. Tum malignum hunc se-
nem, hanc larvam, hanc fabulam, obtruncabo, priusquam ad auxilium ulli procurrant. Simul ipsi Argenidi, Argenidi, inquam. Hæsit miser in cogitati-
one decreti crudelis. Sed quid attinet virgini a-
menti sanguinem mittere? Meliùs flagitij sui memoriâ, & meo vulnere morietur. Aperiam meum
pectus; &, ubi cruore exundabit, injiciam me to-
tum in furiarum omen trepidanti. Nam nisi mori
sic vellem, possem excire meos milites, possem hæc
tecta incolumis in hostium capita effundere. Sed
vivere nolo, ne reconciliari possim Argenidi.

                       Hæc

Hæc & similia furoris consilia agitandi spacium
fuit, dum primæ amoris blanditiæ, Meleandrum,
Archombrotum, atque Argenidem, per cætera-
rum rerum oblivia trahunt. Præcépiſque, & ob-
firmatâ ad facinus mente, jam tangebat capulum,
cùm numina tam fœdè errare insontem non tule-
runt. In ipso igitur articulo, ignarus harum furiarum Meleander, ad illum accedens, Ignosce, inquit, hospes, quòd nos ab officio tui colendi paulis-
per insperata avertit læticia, quam non minùs fortè
gaudebis, quàm me modò & Argenidem vidisti.
Veni mortalium charissime, felicitatis nostræ com-
par, & intellige quid hic dies de te meruerit. Muta-
tus hoc sermone Poliarchus, & in tantâ varietate
affectuum nescius quid expectaret, sentiretve, non
repugnavit ducenti Meleandro. Vbi verò propter
Archombrotum, & Argenidem constitere, tum Meleander jam non adeò pressâ voce, ut circumstan-
tium proximi non audirent; O fœcundum, ait,
hunc diem! O meæ senectuti propitium, quam an-
tea in unâ filiâ acquiescentem, duobus & talibus
liberis auxit! Absit Cœlitum invidia. Quis me
mortalium fortunatior; aut cui preciosius debeat
esse id pauxillum vitæ quod superest? Ergo per tot
ambages, per tot minarum tormenta, erumpens
industria fatorum, hæc mihi præsidia, hæc decora
familiæ parabat? Desine Archombroto irasci, O
hospes, O maxime Regum, & quod utroque præ-
stantius nomen est, Poliarche. Diu est quòd sen-
si odia vestra. Vterque amabatis Argenidem; u-
triusque erit Argenis. Huic enim quam genui,
in sororem affectus durabit. Tibi autem, nisi ali-
ter

ser sentis, eam uxorem despondeo. Nam quòd à
Siciliæ hæreditate excidit, agnito fratre, nihil minùs, ut te novi, aut tu amabis, aut Regina hæc erit.
Quippe Sardinia, & quicquid Radirobanis fuit
(quod deinde & passus es Archombroti esse) hanc
in dotem sequetur. Ita mecum filius meus consti-
tuit. Tu Archombrote prior omnem inimicitiam
ejura; & Regi Poliarcho sororem tuam trade.

Putasset hoc quisquam ? Archombroto conci-
liatore, dextrámque puellæ admovente, invitaba-
tur ad Argenidis nuptias Poliarchus, qui in tali fortunæ ludo cunctabatur credere se esse felicem. E-
rubescebat quoque Argenis; & modò dum obsta-
bant votis bella, vel pater; tam viriliter audax, tam
propè contumax in parentem, & sequutura Poliarchum quocunque juberet; nunc facilibus rebus, se
virginem esse meminerat. Poliarchus simul virgini
manum dare, simul gratias agere Meleandro; eti-
ámque mirari quâ ratione Archombrotus tam su-
bitò evasisset Argenidis frater. Tum, ut fit in mag-
nis & repentinis rebus, omnes sine ordine, simúl-
que loquebantur. Redibat juvenibus mutua inter
se gratia, quam olim auspicati apud Timocleam fu-
erant. Senex cum virgine receperat spiritum; &
Principum alacritas se in intuentes diffundebat.
Stabant nunc Proceres silentio defixi, nunc confusis inter se vocibus aulam implebant. Plures quoque ad famam intraverunt. Nec ingrata Meleandro
frequentia fuit. Nam tantas res, támque publicas,
ab omnibus sciri intererat. Itaq; clara voce, quám-
qui ì sene impetus gaudij fortius pulsabat; Optimi cives, inquit, & hospites, quos hic dies in mul-
tiplicis

tiplicis foederis sanctitatem coegit ; Agite omnes,
gratamini Regibus vestris, & quod superest lucis
inter sacra impendite. Venire in crastinum univer-
sos jubeo ad aulæ vestibulum. Illic & populus præterea & milites implebunt concionem, ne quis deorum consilia ignoret, qui nescio an aliis unquam
verius quàm nobis indulserint. Vos tamen & cen-
seo æquum jam nunc compendio tanta gaudia
præcipere. Comperi Archombrotum ex me geni-
tum esse: Hunc mihi uxor inscio peperit. Regi autem Poliarcho filia mea nubet. Ite læti, & omnium
pulcherrimum diem, si lubet, pervigilio vocate. E-
go interim cum genero & filio quæ in rem sunt,
constituam.

Sic dimissis Proceribus, Poliarchum in interio-
rem regiæ partem duxit, eâ vesperâ inter charissi-
morum consortia exultaturus. Quæ tum vota sin-
gulorum, qui sensus fuere ? Castissimæ Argenidi
aderat fructus constantiæ ; pervicerátque tot maliæ,
ne quà videretur optimâ sorte dignior esse. Poliarcho jam æmulationis, jam ægritudinis oblito, ju-
cundissimum erat traduci soceri risu, quòd osculis
invidisset quæ Argenis Archombroto sororiâ cha-
ritate posuerat. Vtrumque præterea Meleander ri-
debat, nunc generum Archombrotum, nunc Poliarchum Theocrinem vocando. Et ab Argenide
quærebat Archombrotus, quid se agnito lætata po-
tissimùm esset ; an quòd fratrem se haberet ; an
quòd sponsum non esset habitura ? Inter hos jo-
cos, vix quicquam negociis permittebat hilaritas.
Ipse Aneroestus supercilium posuerat, audebátque
lætari ; & quamquam in subhorridâ veste, Regis in
modum

modum à Meleandro & Argenide colebatur. Pauci erant ex secretiori cohorte amicorum tantæ re-
missionis conscij. Tamen Aneroestus, Ibburranes,
Dunalbius, cum Regibus cœnauerunt. Gelanórus,
Arsidas, Gobryásque intererant, Maurúsque Ali-
cipsa, & Cum Cleobulo Eurymedes, Nicopompus
bis à Rege vocatus paulò serius venit. Nam conden-
do epithalamio secesserat. Vnà porrò ex Matronis
Timoclea Argenidem comitabatur. Hi propemo-
dum soli Regibus ad eam cœnam ministri fuere. Et
omnibus quidem præcipuus de Poliarcho erat ser-
mo, vt amasset, vt tanquam suæ sortis oblitus adiis-
set pericula, ignotus, prodigus sui, nec à fortunà
nec ab hostibus tutus. Vnde is ardor, quæve initia
ad tantæ constantiæ amorem fuissent! Ille verò a-
uidissimè audientibus referebat; se de Argenidis
formà atque virtutibus multa inaudisse in Gallià;
hinc subiectos iuuenili animo stimulos, quos tantæ indolis admiratio, aut verius ipsa fata sensim au-
xerunt ; Ac cùm sciret spem connubij Siculis legibus intercisam, quæ Gallicas damnabant nuptias,
hoc velut obice irritatam cupiditatem acrius exar-
sisse ; Et se quidem simulatà pietate in deos exter-
nos quasi eorum templa peteret ; solum cum
Gelanoro nauigauisse in Siciliam, eo consilio vt
præsens agnosceret essetne par famæ Argenis, &
eo bello digna quod ipse in Siculas leges medita-
batur ; si illà, vt aliquando fore sperabat ; obse-
quiis suis demerità, ex solæ morarentur felicita-
tem suam ; Cùm verò Siciliam intrauit, ne vsurpa-
re quidem oculis virginem licuisse, quam scilicet
munimentis arcis inclusam nefas, erat à viris
                                                    tunc

tunc conspici. Hinc felicissimæ temeritatis consili-
um se sumpsisse, vt muliebri stolâ virginem simula-
ret, vt Selenissæ imponeret, appellaretúrque Theocrine. Cætera narraturum adiuuit Meleander, inte-
risum stuporémque repetens memoriâ, quàm, ille
omniâ similis puellæ venisset; quàm lachrima-
bili fabulâ elicuisset misericordiam suam; aditúm-
que inuenisset ad Argenidem; quâ denique virtute,
quo robore, domuisset Sicarios qui in arcem intra-
uerant, & de Theocrine facta Pallas fuisset.

A Poliarcho deinde ad Archombrotum sermone traducto, plurima quoque in eo mirabantur.
Ergo ille debebatur Siciliæ Princeps, insciúfque
quem coleret Meleandrum amauerat! Vt diu Hyæ-
nisbe habuisset rem secretam! vt tempori retexis-
set! quàm similem repertis ad aurium voluptatem
commentis dij hunc contextum rerum dedissent!
Eos interim docebat Meleander suûm in Africâ
conjugium; & quantum fas erat per præsentem læticiam, ingemiscebat vxori defunctæ: sæpiúsque, &
per partes cuncta narrando, ea ipsa digerebat quæ
postridie in concione dissereret.

Multùm noctis processerat, cùm à cœna reces-
sum est. Vbi prope ortum sol fuit, quotquot Pa-
normi erant, impediti frondibus caput, confluxe-
runt ad regiam. Angusta multitudini atria erant.
Hi in muros euasere, aut subitaria theatra impleue-
runt. Alij applicuerant scalas, quibus plus iusto o-
neratis, haud paucæ defluxerunt in subiectos. Ad
ipsas palatij fores, exiguæ scenæ species penè ad al-
titudinem hominis attollebatur. Illic Regum sug-
gestus eminebant; duo quidem fronte æquali quibus

bus Poliarchus & Meleander federunt, Totidem
paulò interiùs ad latus recefferant, Archombroto
Argenidíque ornati. Poftquam Reges præbuere fe
populo, & præco plaufum compefcuit; nonnihil
motatus Meleander; Si quid ominofum, inquit,
afferrem, (optimi hofpites, atque cives) arte aliquâ
effet opus, & veluti condimento, quo illud apud
veftra mitigarem ingenia. Nunc quid opus eft anxiâ
eloquentiâ conmendare deorum munera, quæ ip-
fi tantopere ornarunt? Affero vobis læticiam, Regibus gentibúfque pacem ac fœdera; hoftibus noftri
nominis pavorem, tumultus, exitium.   Nec vos
præco hæc ipfa ad quæ audienda conveniftis igno-
rare. Aliquis deus, & ipfa fi quod numen habet fa-
ma, haud dubiè fparfit in vobis celebrare hunc diem filiæ meæ nuptiis cum Rege Poliarcho, & veluti altero natali filii mei (flexáque cervice in affir-
gentem Archombrotum refpexit.)   Quem cur
tamdiu ignorarim, cur nunc demum agnoverim,
operæ precium erit (cives) & vos quoque cognof-
cere. Accipe Reginæ Mauritaniæ literas, Præco,
& quantum voce vales publicè recita.
  Tum præco traditam epiftolam in hunc modum
exorfus eft. Regina Hyanisbe Regi Meleandro falu-
tê. Tuâ virtute an vitio dicam factum, ut ante hunc
diem, non cenferem gaudium tibi dandum; quo
nunc mirantê impertiar? Nam & vitio duco, quòd
cum Anna meâ forore nuptias me celatam voluifti,
nec deinde eâ extinctâ quæfifti, an inde tibi aliquid
fupereffet. Virtutem porrò tuam fic colui, ut trade-
re tibi ftirpê noluerim, nifi experimento priùs cap-
to an te digna adolefceret. Nunc cùm omnia ge-
                                                   ner

fieri confentiant, aperiendum eft quod tot annis a-
pud me continui. Cùm fororem meam Annam tibi occultis nuptam aufpiciis, apud nos reliquiffes
in tuam Siciliam iturus, effluxifféntque menfes quibus ipfa crefcentem uterum varia arte celavit; tandem cœpit atriter ægrotare. Nos alium morbum
ratæ inutilia ferebamus remedia. Sed illa mortis o-
men concipiens, ita me folam affata eft. Ignofce;
mea foror, non aliam deprecanti quam filentii cul-
pam. Meleandri Siciliæ Regis uxor fum. In partu
jám laboro; nec incolumis, nifi dolores fallunt, e-
nitar. Si quid ex me natum vivet, tuum arbitri-
um efto, foror, vel alere, vel patri tranfmittere. Mal-
lem tamen fecretum affervari, ne me populus ma-
trem prius quàm nuptam intelligat. Cæterúm fup-
primendi fœderis noftri caufæ variæ fuerunt; tum
quòd Numidam Cyrthum, importunum mihi procum, & vi forte ufurum, metuebamus; tum quòd
Meleander regia pompa, quam ornaturus difceffit,
fibi me jungi concupiit; deníque miferam me pu-
dor tenebat, quem heu timeo etiamnum & loquen-
do ne violem. En, foror, ad pulvinum conjugii leges ipfius Meleandri ttianu fcriptæ, quibus & egó
eo nomine appofito addidi fidem. (fimúlque ta-
bellas tradidit) In ifta autem pyxide funt arcanorum
noftrorum confciæ notæ; aliquot literæ annulí-
que, & ex utriúfque crine armilla. Cùm hæc often-
det, fciet me tibi omnem rem credidiffe. In ipfo fer-
mone vocem amifit. Ego refectam folatæ, paucas fi-
diffimarum matronarum advocavi; & fedulò quæ
neceffaria erant curavimus. Sed vincebat arte dolor.
Peperit tamen filium, quem oculis viventis admovimus.

S s   Petii

Petii deinde, an cogere vires posset ad breviſſimam
ſcriptionem; neſcio quo numine ad res quas hodie agimus jam tum meam curam inſtituente. Fecit
illa, & in tabellis exaravit ſe mori, ſe filium tuum
mihi relinquere. Agnoſces manum illius (ô Rex)
quamvis literas malè ductas morbi tremor con-
fuderit. Nec multò pòſt inter meos complexus ex-
tincta eſt. Quatuor omnino matronæ mecum e-
rant. Ego cuidam Sophonemæ, cui apud me po-
tiſſimùm fides erat, infantem permitto; ageret e-
jus curam; nutricem inveniret ignaram quem ale-
ret. Verita quoque ne quid ex tot conſcius ullæ ef-
funderet, per eandem deinde Sophonemem cæte-
ras fallo, ut crederent infantem obiiſſe. Inter eoſ-
dem dies frater Iuba decedens reliquit mihi regnum;
& vir Syphax, ſatis quodam agmine in nos ruen-
tibus, vitâ functus eſt. Ego tot luctibus plena, non
tui Meleander, non ſororis oblita ſum. Prægnan-
tem me fingo; deinde poſthumum edere mentı-
or, adjuvante eâdem Sophoneme. Supponi
tunc mihi tuus non potuit. Nam non conveniſſet
tot menſium infans puerperæ. Sed commodum foe-
tum Sophoneme cunis inſeruit; quem deinde meo
juſſu alendum abvexit; Ego ſimulans faſcini me-
tum, vetui ne quis ultra nutrices, unámque Sophonemem, filium meum inſpiceret. Ita biennio
circumacto facile fuit Hyempſalem tuum (ita moriens mater appellavit de nomine avi) tanquam
ex me natum oſtendere. Huic me deinceps; huic
& regnum ſervavi. Nullæ me impulere ad nuptias
vicinorum Regû preces. Poſtquâ annorum viginti
trium fuit, apud illum commendavi virtute
cuæ

tuæ: hortata sum, ut in rudimentum regnandi ad
te profectus, animum suum formaret ex tuo. Et
hæc facilius effecturum si omitteret suæ fortunæ insignia, nec pro matre me jactaret; Ne indulgentia
tua, & cæterorum adulatio, crudam illam veram-
que virtutem auferret, quæ sæpe Principibus viris
negata, privatorum discrimina & fortunam nobi-
litat. Obsequens dicto ivit, & mirum est adeo pla-
cuisse, ut magnus Rex filiam novissimo conjugio
susceptam & in quâ liberorum summam tibi crede-
bas, ei velles despondere. Cùm id mihi nunciasset,
quamquam illius virtute & genio tuo læta, qui fe-
cerat ut adhuc ignotum filium amares; tamen ad
incestarum nuptiarum omen expavi, ne frater
sorori jungeretur. Adhuc me alia pericula ter-
rebant; Radirobane in Africæ perniciem cum
exercitu veniente. Igitur nostro Hiempsali, quem
Archombrotum appellatis, ita scripsi, ut nuptias
jam apud vos ut audio constitutas differrem; & ipse ad auxilium meum accitus cum classe veni-
ret. Sera tamen fuissent auxilia, nec invenisset
quam juvaret, ni Regem Poliarchum cum Gal-
lorum suorum exercitu nobis tempestas dedisset.
Hujus virtute, opima Radirobanis in Martis
nostri templo sunt. Sed penè tristiora fuere apud
nos pace quàm bello discrimina: Poliarcho atque Hyempsale sævissimâ æmulatione ardentibus.
Causa odii tua Argenis; cujus nuptias uterque su-
pra humanæ cupiditatis morem ambit. Intellecto
filii tui errore, ab iis impetravi, ne prius furiosa lis
ad ferrum perveniret, quàm tibi tradidissent has
literas. Illico utrumque voti compotem fore;

Quod

Quod ita demum erit, si tuum filium agnosces, &
Poliarcho Regi, quo propior factis deorum, & virtutibus, hodie nemo vivit, filiam tuam dabis uxorem. Dotem ex tuis vel meis rebus ei dicas permitto. Sicilia, Mauritania, recénsque incrementum
Sardiniæ, satis erunt, ut & filius opulentissimè reg-
net; & gnata pro genere & sorte collocetur. Mitto
in arculâ quicquid arcani mihi soror moriens reliquit; inter cætera ultimas ad te literas, quibus se superstite filio extingui significat. Quæ omnia ipso
hoc anno tantum non perierunt. Arculam, proh
nefas, rapuerant peiratæ. Sed Rex Poliarchus cæ-
sis latronibus mihi inviolatam restituit. Ita pro par-
te huic etiam filium tuum debes; debeo ego regnum, jamdiu tuo Hyempsali destinatam. Præter
Argenidem nihil ad hæc operæ mercedis est. Vale,
& felicitate quam dij faciunt senium tuum oblecta.
    Longissimas literas raucus præco vix absolvit.
Lectionem confusæ in populo voces sequutæ sunt.
Plerique audierant, alij quærendo rogandóque pe-
nitus turbabant. Multis quoque literæ erant ob-
scuræ; quod futurum haud dubius Meleander, coe-
pit has ipsas aliâ oratione exponere. Historiam
suæ juventutis repetiit; ut patre jubente uxorem
olim duxisset Brutiorum Principis filiam, quæ sex-
ennio nupta ac sterilis, decesserat ex vulnere, quod
de equo inter venandum lapsa in stipite accepit.
Tunc se tricesimum quintum ætatis annum egisse,
patre adhuc superstite. Eâdem tempestate regnasse
in Mauritaniâ Iubam Siciliæ amicum, ad quem cû
paucis comitibus profectus est, avertendi luctûs
causâ, quem mors uxoris faciebat. Deinde memo-
                                                rabū

rabat duas sorores Iubæ fuisse. Seniorem Hyanisbem, Syphaci, potenti illic viro collatam ; Annam
juniori nomen fuisse, eámque habuisse ex Numi-
diá procum, qui Cyrthus dicebatur, tantarum viri-
um hominem, at hunc Iuba, quamvis sibi non pro-
batum, timeret offendere. Se interim Annæ amore
correptum ; virginíque illum Numidam exoso pla-
cuisse. Secretis ergo fœderibus consensisse utrumque in nuptias ; eáque admonénte contrahendas
ex Siciliá vires priusquam huic Numidæ palàm
obstaret, se navigasse in patriam ; Et illic; ne pro-
misso tempore in Africam rediret, patris funere fuisse tardatum. Inter has moras de Annæ interitu
audivisse, & omissá Mauritaniá amavisse Siculam
virginem, patruo suo genitam ; ex quá nata erat Argenis. Cætera ex Hyanisbes epistolá habetis, Optimi cives, ut Ipsa fratri Iubæ in regnum successerit,
ut hunc mihi filium Anna pepererit. Veri pignora
in obsignatá arculá misit ; mihi quidem maximo
præteritarum rerum sensu recognita.

Tum in Poliarchum intuitus ; Te verò, maxime Regum, inquit, quo nomine compellem ; cujus munus est quòd vivimus, quódque regnamus?
Tu me vinculis, tu Argenidem exemisti, cùm in
Gynecæo Lycogenis mancipia furerent. Tu in a-
cie meis militibus præivisti ad victoriam iter ; denique unus hostes fudisti. Inde meo heu malo, &
quicquid excuses dedecore, excessisti Siciliá. Nec
contumeliæ nostræ tuam bonitatem vicerunt. Læ-
sus quoque amavisti Argenidem. Quid dicam te
indicia per quæ ego ad filij notitiam, ille ad pa-
trem perveniret, invenisse diis ducentibus apud

pei-

peiratas, & virtute fervaviffe? In Africæ autem non
triumphare Radirobanem quantæ molis res fuerit;
nondum toto fanguine reparato, in tuo vultu pal-
lor oftendit. Vtinam nomen amares quod me tibi fubmitteret. Socerum dici mavis. Fælicem Argenidem in tanta fœdera ituram. Tu quidem tui
virtute damnafti nimis formidolofam majorum
noftrorum folertiam, qui ad Gallicam magnitudi-
nem adeò expavere, ut Siculis Principibus interdi-
cerent conjugia veftra ; quafi tanta affinitas fervitu-
tis inftar effet. Meruifti ut confenfu publico anti-
quemus omnes hanc legem. Sed & dij fecerunt,
ne opus fit ab ejufmodi fanctione recedere. Filium enim ad quem Sicilia perveniat, mihi reftitue-
runt. Meam autem Argenidem fortuna non infe-
rior, Sardinia cum Liguribus manet ; quæ regna
nihil vetantibus legibus noftris tuæ Galliæ adjun-
get. Hic Archombrotus, uti convenerat, pacem
patris petiit ad dicendum. Mox ita Poliarcho. Sardiniæ poffeffio, quam habeo, inquit, quid eft aliud
quàm victoriæ tuæ fructus? Eam debellafti in A-
fricâ. Veni ego ad triumphum. Tu ergo, chariffi-
ma foror, tu quam à me fuiffe amatam vel ipfe Poliarchus ignofcit, fume regium infigne, & pro fpe
Siciliæ, in quam me natalium jura inferuere, terra-
rum omnium quæ fub Radirobane fuerunt, efto
Regina. Feres ad virum, quod ipfe victoriæ jure
ferre potuerat. Simul diadema Sorori impofuit;
flente quidem præ læticiæ copiâ Meleandro; populo autem tantis acclamationibus rem probante,
vt diutiffimè auribus vfus abfuerit. Poliarchus et
eloquentiâ pollebat, ita cœpit beneficiorum fuo-
rum

rum memoriam eleuarê, vt folerter augeret ; reue-
rentiſſimus Meleandri ; Archombroto, Argenidi,
populo blandus ; vt dubium eſſet arma an pacem
magis deceret.

Iámque omnibus ad templum proceſſuris, filius
Nicopompi vix decennium egreſſus, patre ducen-
te ſe admovit Argenidi, blandéque epithalamium à
patre conditum tradens, ſe illius authorem non in-
eptâ aut timidâ jocoſitate aſſeruit. Cúmque eum
Meleander vocaſſet, ſibi & Poliarcho juſſit ejuſdem
carminis exemplaria donari, quæ puer præparatâ
manu tenebat ; rogandóque cuius opus hoc eſſet,
ſæpiùs adegit ridentem mentiri. Pauci verſus, ut ad
Principes, & occupatos, erant ; ideóque & plures
à quibus legerentur habuere.

Lapſus ab aſtrifero feſta ad connubia cœlo
Phœbus adeſt. Vos, O Superi, vos cernere coràm
Poſſumus Aoniy Vates. En panditur æther,
Et longo in noſtras deſcenditis ordine terras.
Dúmq́, faces accendit Hymen, dato Numine pompam
Exornat Regina deûm, parvuſq́, Cupido
Lene facit vultus, nullóque exerrat in ictu ;
Ecce coronat à plectrum teſtudine ducens,
Sic pulcher roſeo Latonius inchoat ore.

Iungite concordes manſura in fœdera dextras,
Quæ non ulla dies, quæ non fata impia rumpant,
Iungite io Reges. Blandis lux aurea ſurgit
Auſpiciis ; Hymenæus adeſt ; Date laurea ſerta
Poſtibus, & quinos fax pronuba ſurgat in ignes.
Gallica Trinacrios iungunt ſibi numina divos.
O ſocer! O ſponſi! Speratáque turba nepotum!

Aſpice nunc felix promiſſa virginis ora.

Palladijs hęc forma genis ; has alma nitentes
Fert Cytherea comas ; tali Saturnia regnat
Lumine, vulnificos vel cùm Latonia cinctus
Exit, eq. sua magnum petit ethera syluis.
Talis sponsa venit : Tu divûm hęc munera, Princeps,
Cuncta vide ; mentisque bonis tamen acrius omne
Fige animi lumen ; mortalia corda puella
Esse neges, sortesque tuas aquabis Olympo.
Illa etiam vultusq; tuos, auroq; nitentem
Gesariem, & castu vibrantia lumina flammis,
Cernere gaudet amans ; & tunc te mente sub alta
Effingis; qualisq; sævis quatere ardua bellis
Arma soles; nunc quantus eris patria agmina quando
Occanus restitui; parihq; invecta triumpho
Ipsa per effusas tecum spectabitur urbes.
Iamq; timet, ne saeua ferant hęc gaudia venti
Quæ cernit, redeatq; novis insomnia curis.
Ah ne, virgo, time: Non hęc efficta sopore
Leticia est, cupideve errant ludibria mentis.
Certa vides. Adsit genialia numina mecum.
Stat cunctis mens una deus, vox omnibus una ;
Iungite concordes mansura in fœdera d.xtras;
Iungite io dextras, tu formosissima virgo,
Tuq; viros inter quales sub nocte serena
Purpureus socia extinguit Lucifer ignes.
At tu sancta veni, tuaeneraq; merentibus adsis,
Exorata Quies. Satis exhausere pericli,
Sat pigras perpessa moras insignia Regum
Pectora ; nunc votis expectatoq; fruuntur
Connubio. Sic & Tagus hęc astra subire
Non nisi bis sitis potius mercede laboris.
Iungite concordes mansura in fœdera dextras,

Iungite iô dextras. Quò tandem nubila rerum
Et fœdi cessere dies? En serius astra
Ridet, & ingenti cumulavit sua dona favore
Cælicola, O nunquam tranquilla exordia satis
Heroum eximys, nec denique naufraga virtus?

Paratæ ad Iunonis Lucinæ delubrum victimæ
erant; Auguréfque & Pontificum ordo, nuptiis o-
men facturi. Populus viam hymenæo, aut præmia
celebrabat: Et quia Argenidi mater non erat, quæ
facem nubenti filiæ luceret, is Timocleæ honos;
Poliarchi & Archombroti commendatione colla-
tus est. Inuocatis genialibus diis; tædísque præcipuè ignium qui velatæ Argenidi præferebantur;
cùm iam in victimas caderet ferrum, Poliarchus fa-
crorum ministros jubet subsistere, dicíque leuior
augustior ita Archombroto loquutus est. Si fas est
mihi apud te fidem esse, ô frater, doleo me marito
adhuc matronam te quærere. Mihi soror est vultu
& indole quæ vel ignobilem commendaret; annorum plus minùs viginti. Si solida fœdera inter nos
placent, hanc tibi iure fraterno despondebo. Et
quoniam ritu gentili nulla pars regni in eam cade-
re potest; dos erit talenta sexcenta præsentia. Meleander sermonis erat arbiter qui Archombrotum
non tam cunctantem assentiri (nam placebat affinitas) quàm ius patri facientem vt de nuru statue-
ret, interrogauit an eam sibi his legibus pactam vel-
let. Argenidem quoque, quamquam inter vere-
cunda tunc sacra silentium tenentem, monuerat
Poliarchus, vt fratrem in mutua fœdera solicitaret.
Ille se conditionem accipere apertissimo vultu re-
spondit; amplexúfque Poliarchum; Præcepisti
mea

mea vota, fortissime Regum. Quis te deus in mei
animi secreta perduxit? Ergo hæc etiam sacra mihi
absentem coniungent. Tu fidem charissime, vtrim-
que præstabis. Admoniti sacerdotes vt geminarent
auspicia, sedulitate eximiâ circa templum omnia
turbabant; Cúmque res emanasset in populum,
nouo gratulantium clamore plenus aër præteruo-
lantes aliquot aues intercepto alarum officio exani-
mauit. Omnes plaudebant. Omnes erant bacchan-
tium lætitiæ proximi; Cœtúque confuso, nullâ
discrimine ordinum tanta gaudia meminerant.

Diis interim profecta dabantur: & cùm hostiæ,
quarum vna victrici iecoris fuit, placuissent Haruspi-
ci; thure accenso Sponsi in fœdera nuptiarum ad
aram subiere. Perpetratis denique sacris, iam pompa vertebatur ad regiam, cùm in templi vestibulo
Anaroestus occurrit discessuris, pallido vultu, & di-
uinandi stimulis pleno. Nam meritum pectus numina insederant. Igitur quassans emotum deorum
furoribus caput, Saluete, inquit, O Reges, O nu-
minum cura, exerciti hactenus satis, nunc eorun-
dem clementiâ experturi nihil virtute iucundius.
Fœlicissime senum, ah ne diis exprobra, Meleander, istos annos inter bella scelúsque tuorum ciui-
um consumptos. Viuida ætas, annísque adhuc plu-
rimis suffectura, nihil publicè, nihil domi time-
bit. Nunc in Africâ videbis Hyanisbem, nunc in
Siciliâ illam excipies. Procul mala factionum, procul insidiatorum atrocitas. Vestrum senium, iuuen-
túsque Archombroti, reuerentiâ & errore subiget
omnes; Hunc triumphantem felix pater de pro-
ximis Brutiis, Lucanísque, & Epeirei littore aspi-
cies;

cies; huius pignora in veſtris adoleſcent amplexi-
bus, longam Principum feriem datura Siciliæ;
Nec charior tibi gnata nunc Galliæ deſtinata, quàm
quæ inde nurus aduenfet. At vos ſæculi gemmæ,
tu Poliarche, túque Argenis, ne hîc fidei, hîc vir-
tutum præmia quæ certa vos manent, expectetis
audire. Multa ignoro; multa filenda funt. Fata ipſa felicitatis partem in quam producti eſtis, deos
celant, ne illi vobis inuideant. Pauca tamen de
multis accipite. Qui vos amor hodie iungit, ad ſe-
nium inuiolatos deducet. Non eum iurgia, non
faſtidia, non ægrarum ſuſpicionum cura libabit.
Proferetis imperij fines. Hinc vos Rhenus, hinc O-
ceanus victores aſpiciet. Timandræ inter nepotum
cuneos exultantis imagines, ſæpe pro Cybele bo-
nus poſteritatis error accipiet. Gloriam veſtram,
fortitudinem, nutus, ſuſpicient vicinæ latè gentes;
Non abnuent vinci, non regi. Si quò ibitis, ipſa
vos falus feret. quicquid optabitis, dij vota præ-
uenient. Ac ne felicitas mortem deſtituat; nox v-
na feſſos fenio exoluet, plura mox aſtra exhi-
bitura mortalibus. Nec de famâ dubita-
te. Hanc præſtabit æternam hiſtoriæ
genius, quam in gentibus o-
lim ſparſam nulla vis,
nulla ætas ex-
tinguet.

FINIS.

The selection from *Histoire de Poliarque et d'Argenis* (1624) is reproduced, by permission, from the copy in the Rare Book Collection, The University of North Carolina at Chapel Hill (shelfmark PR2209/B35/A714/ 1624). The text block of the original measures 133 × 74 mm.

Pages 169–174 are misnumbered as 199–207.

Readings where the copy is blotted:

167.4   ciuilité: Poliarque

167.8   nesie: le More est

168.16   prit la parole

HISTOIRE
DE POLIARQVE
ET D'ARGENIS.

Par F. N. Coeffeteav, *Euesque de Marseille.*

A PARIS.

Chez {
Samvel Thibovst,
&
Iaqves Villery, au
Palais.

M. DC. XXIV.
Auec Priuilege du Roy.

ries qui estoient dedans
estoient d'vn pris ine-
stimable, mais ce n'e-
stoit pas le secret. Apres
auoir pris congé de la
Royne, les deux flottes
des Princes ennemis se
mettét à la voile sans que
nul d'eux monstre aucun
signe de son courroux
contre son riual; Ils arri-
uent presque à mesme
temps à la Cour de Me-
leandre. Argenis a aduis
que son Poliarque est si
prés d'elle ; Ceste ioyé

l'euſt tranſportée, mais le
dépit ſe ietta à la trauerſe,
lors qu'elle euſt appris
qu'il auoit fait ſon pere
arbitre de ſon mariage.
Eſt-ce donc là, dit-elle,
l'eſtat qu'il fait de moy, de
ſe mettre ainſi au hazard
de me perdre? Et ſi mon
Pere qui incline du coſté
du More me donne à luy,
penſe-t'il que i'y conſen-
te iamais: Deuant que ce-
la m'arriue, ou le fer, ou le
poiſon m'oſteront du
monde; l'auray plus de

G v

courage que luy; ma mort
abattra tous les trophées
que ce More se va dref-
fant en son esprit; & feray
voir à Poliarque que ie
sçay aymer plus constam-
ment & plus fidelement
que luy. Au moins si mon
fexe m'ôfte le moyen de
disputer côtre luy la gloire des armes, rié ne m'em-
pefchera de rauir celle de
la constance. Cefte lice eft
ouuerte à tous les bons
courages fans diftinction
de fexe, & ie ne feray pas

la premiere fille qui aura
surpassé les hommes en fi-
delité.

Cependant les deux
Amants sont fauorable-
ment reçeus à la Cour, ou
Poliarque commence à
reprendre son lustre , &
comme à ternir vn peu la
gloire du Prince de Mau-
ritanie : ils vont faire la
reuerence au Roy, qui
leur fait tout le bon ac-
cueil qu'ils eussent peu
desirer à ce premier
abord. Poliarque fit son

G vj

compliment le premier
en peu de paroles. Mais le
More ayant presenté les
lettres & l'Fscrin dont sa
mere l'auoit chargé pour
les donner à Meleandre,
se vid engagé à vn plus
long entretien.

A l'ouuerture des let-
tres le Roy changea de
couleur les ayant leuës
fort exactement & auec
vne extraordinaire atten-
tion, il prit vne petite
clef d'or que la Royne de
Mauritanie auoit enfer-

mée dedans, & en ouurir
l'Escrin, où il trouua des
choses qui partagerent
tellement son esprit que
parmy les signes qu'il
donna de son contente-
ment on vid les larmes
couler de ses yeux en tel-
le abondance que toute
la compagnie en demeu-
ra estonnée. A mesme
temps oubliant vn peu ce
qui estoit de la ciuilité, il
laissa seul le Prince de
France, & tira à part le
More comme pour l'en-

tretenir plus priuement
& auec plus de liberté;
ceste negligence ne fust
rien au prix de ce qui sui-
uit; Le tenant à l'escart il
se ietta à son col, l'em-
brasse, le baise, & luy
dóne les plus sésibles tes-
moignages qu'il eust peu
souhaitter de son affectió.
Non contant de cela,
il euuoya querir à grand
haste sa fille, à qui en arri-
uant il dit tout bas quel-
ques paroles accópagnée
d'vne action qui sembloit

eftre vne image de la
ioye de fon cœur. La
Princeffe fans regarder
ce qui eftoit fi prés d'elle,
s'aduance pour faluer le
More auec de vifibles
marques d'amour, Poliar-
que demeure efperdu de
ce fpectacle, & ne fçait
plus quelle contenance
tenir, mais iugeant par la
bonne chere qu'Argenis
faifoit à Archombrot
que toutes fes efperances
eftoient ruinées, & que
fon riual alloit triom-

pher de ſes pourſuites, ſe
laiſſa aller au deſeſpoir,
& dans l'amertume de ſes
penſées ſe priſt à dire en
ſon ame, Eſt-ce donc là le
fruiĉt de tant de peines
que i'ay priſes, & tant de
hazards que i'ay courus
pour m'aſſeurer des bon-
nes graces de ce prodige
d'inconſtance, celle que
les plus violentes rigueurs
d'vn pere & mille marty-
res ne deuoient point ny
flechir, ny eſbranler, ſe
laiſſe ſurprendre à vne

petite flatterie que ce
Vieillard luy dit à l'oreil-
le : Quelles montagnes
d'or ? quelles eternelles
sources de felicité luy
a t'on peu promettre
pour changer ainsi son
courage, & alterer son esprit? malheureuse Roy-
ne de Mauritanie, reiect-
tó de ses vieilles souches,
quels characteres & quels
enchantements as-tu faits
sur ces lettres pour leur
imprimer la force &
leur donner la puissance

de causer vn si mōstrueux
changemēt, & de ruiner
en si peu d'heure ce que
i'auois basty auec vne si
longue patience ; que ie
sois puny de l'imprudēce
que i'ay commise, me fiāt
aux paroles d'vne femme
& aux promesses d'vne
fille, dont les ruses & la
legereté, qualitez insepa-
rables de ce sexe, me de-
uoient rendre la foy plus
suspecte que celle des
vents qui m'ont amené &
poussé dans cet infame

riuage:Mais au fort, si on
a peu tromper Poliar-
que, il en sçaura faire vne
si cruelle vengeance, que
ny les autheurs, ny les cô-
plices de ceste perfidie
n'auront pas grand sujet
d'en bastir des triomphes,
ny d'en dresser des tro-
phées à leur vanité. Ce
detestable Vieillard qui
par les artifices dont il est
plein, s'est tousiours op-
posé à mon contentemêt,
& ces deux insoléts Amás
qui se ioüent du bris de

ma fortune, seront les vi-
ctimes de ma fureur :
Mais ce n'est pas tout, ie
veux aussi mourir , afin
que mon ombre poursui-
ue & persecute ceste in-
gratte Argenis iusqu'au
throsne des Dieux im-
mortels : Deuant qui ie
luy reprocheray sa pro-
digieuse infidelité , que
mille serments conçeus
en leur nom deuoient ar-
rester si elle eust eu le sen-
timent& la creance qu'el-
le deuoit auoir de leurs

puiſſances & de leur iuſti-
ce; il y a apparence que ce
fuſt le bon genie de Po-
liarque, ou l'Ange tute-
laire de la Sicile qui occu-
pa ſon eſprit à ces tragi-
ques penſées, afin de re-
tarder ſon deſſein & de le
diuertir durât autant d'eſ-
pace qu'il en falloit, pour
donner loiſir à Melean-
dre & à Argenis de ſe re-
cognoiſtre, & de luy faire
leurs excuſes. Comme dôc
il eſtoit ſur le point d'aller executer vn ſi furieux

dessein, & d'oster du mō-
de Meleandre, Argenis,
& son riual, pour apres
ceste sanglante execution
se passer aussi l'espée au
trauers du corps, & laisser
par ce moyen de tragi-
ques marques de sa ialou-
sie & de son despit. Ceux
qui sembloient l'auoir
trop negligé s'entrerent
en eux mesmes, & s'ap-
perceuant de leurs fautes,
s'en allerent deuers luy
s'excuser, & luy descou-
urirent le sujet de ceste

ioye, qui les ayant rauis
hors d'eux mesmes, leur
auoit fait oublier toute
ciuilité. Poliarque treuue
dás leurs discours & dans
leurs raisons les charmes
de sa fureur & de sa fre-
nesie. le More estreco-
gneu pour frere d'Arge-
nis, la Royne de Maurita-
nie en auoit descouuert
l'histoire par ses letrres, &
en auoit donné de si bon-
nes marques à Meleandre
qu'il ne pouuoit plus
doubter qu'il ne fust son

fils, & le iuste heritier des
deux Couronnes, de sor-
te qu'Archôbrot recueil-
lant la succession de ces
Estats, laissoit frâchemét
la possession de sa sœur la
Princesse à Poliarque, qui
n'eust pas voulu la chan-
ger auec mille sceptres.
    Méleandre voyant la
plus grande partie de l'assistance n'entendre rien
en ses merueilles, & que
chacun en desireroit vn
plus grâd esclarcissemét,
prit la parole, & faisant
                        vn

vn bref difcours du voya-
ge qu'il auoit fait en Af-
frique durant les ardeurs,
de fa ieuneffe auoüa qu'il,
auoit efté épris d'vne,
beauté de qui s'eftant ac-
quis les bonnes graces, il
l'auoit en fin efpoufée fe-
crettement, & que fes af-
faires l'ayant rappellé en
Sicile, il l'auoit laiffée en-
ceinte d'vn fils qui eftoit
Archombrot, que de-
puis Hyanifbé fe voyant
fans enfans du Roy fon
mary, auroit fuppofé,
H

feignant d'en estre ac-
couchée, qu'elle auroit
esté induite à se faire, par
ce que sa sœur qui estoit
celle qu'il auoit aymée, se
voyant preste de mourir
de ses couches, luy en auroit descouuert le secret.
Partant qu'on ne deuoit
point doubter qu'Ar-
chombrot ne fust frere
d'Argenis, au mariage de
laquelle pour ceste raison
il ne pourroit plus aspi-
rer, mais qu'il en laissoit
la iouïssance libre à Po-
H

liarque, Prince incompa-
rable,& digne de l'alliance de la plus grande Princesse de la terre ; en suite
dequoy si iamais la Sicile
s'estoit veuë au comble
du bon-heur, c'estoit à ce
point où les destins l'a-
uoient conduite par des
moyens indogneus aux
hommes, qu'à ceste occa-
sion donc tout le monde
donnast des signes d'vne
resiouïssance publique,
& que chacun couruft
dans les Teples des Dieux

pour leur rendre milles
actions de graces de tant
de benedictions qu'ils
auoient à mesme temps
respandus sur sa Cou-
ronne. A ces paroles on
eust dit que le peuple
estoit transporté d'vn secret rauissement, tant il
donna de tesmoignage
de sa ioye parmy toutes
les festes, au milieu des sacrifices : Meleandre du
consentement d'Archom-
brot offre à Poliarque le
Royaume de Sardaigne

pour le mariage d'Arge-
nis, Poliarque s'en tenant
merueilleufement con-
tât, fait ouuerture de l'alliance d'vne fienne fœut
fille de Fracè à Archobrot,
qui accepte auec mille
actions de graces ce glo-
rieux party, ainfi les deux
Couronnes de France &
de Sicile demeurent vnies
auec de fi puiffants liens,
qu'il femble que les de-
ftins en vouloient rendre
l'alliance eternelle.

D'autre cofté Poliar-

H iij

que se treuue au comble
de ses desirs, se voyant en
possession de celle qu'il
aymoit plus cherement
que sa vie ; Certes comme
les rigueurs d'vn long hy-
uer font treuuer le prin-
temps plus agreable, aussi
toutes ses trauerses qu'il
auoit soufferres en ce-
ste recherche luy en fi-
rent trouuer la iouïssan-
ce plus douce.

FIN.

The selection from *Barclay his Argenis*, tr. Kingsmill Long, 2nd edition (1636, *STC* 1392.5) is reproduced, by permission, from the Folger Shakespeare Library (shelfmark *STC* 1395, copy 2), with the title page and page 719 substituted, by permission, from the Newberry Library copy (shelfmark Case Y682 B24). The text block of the original measures 171 × 101 mm.

Readings where the Folger copy is blotted:

699.4   was come of dif-

699.5   both of them made a

699.13   each of them ex-

714.28   forward to the Temple

BARCLAY his ARGENIS,
or, The Loves of
POLYARCHUS
& ARGENIS.
Faithfully Translated out
of Latin into English.
by
KINGSMILL LONG
Esquire.
The Second Edition;
Beautified with Pictures
Together with a Key
Præfixed to unlock
the whole Story.

London Printed for Henry Seile
at the Signe of the Tygres head
in Fleetstreet ———— neere the
Conduit. 1636.

CHAP. XVIII.

Hyanisbe's *Letter presented to* Meleander. Poliarchus *much troubled.* Archombrotus *discovered to be the Sonne of* Meleander.

Ow were they entred the Court, and *Meleander* invited them to sit downe in Chayres of Estate, and there to discourse together. But they thinking now the time was come of dispatching their businesse, both of them made a strand, and *Archombrotus* presenting his Mothers Letters to *Meleander*, requested him presently to peruse them: for, till then, he might take no rest at all. *Poliarchus* made the same request. The King wondring what businesse of such hasty dispatch these Letters might containe; breakes up the Seale, and begins to reade them. And presently *Poliarchus* and *Archombrotus* begun to discover in their lookes evident tokens of disquiet thoughts: for each of them expected from those Letters their certaine fate. If the businesse should fall out otherwise then *Hyanisbe* had promised; if eyther there should be no meanes offered of friendship betweene them, or but ill conditions, they hartned themselves on to the fight, and could thinke of nothing but the sword and fury. *Archombrotus* also, with the Letters, delivered *Meleander* the Cabbinet, (so his Mother had willed him) that *Poliarchus* had brought backe from the Pyrates. Neyther had *Meleander* read much of the Letter, when like a man distraught, he one while talkes to himselfe, another while casts his eyes upon *Archombrotus*, and then falls to the Letter againe, and to stop at every Sentence. There was a small key inclosed in the Letter, wherewith the Cabbinet was to be unlocked, which the King holding fast in his hand, continued reading the Letter. *Poliarchus* and *Archombrotus*

brotus now no longer doubted, but these powerfull Letters contained matter of very great consequence. At last, *Meleander* withdrew himselfe to a Table by the next wall, and takes speciall survey himselfe alone, of what was contained in the Cabbinet he had now opened. Some letters there were, which with sighs and teares he kissed, when he had read them over : and a Ring, with some private tokens of secret businesse, which made the old man give beliefe to what *Hyanisbe* had written.

So, being surprized with the extremity of passion, he requests *Poliarchus* to give him leave to goe on with some important and secret businesse; and withall, takes the wondring *Archombrotus* more familiarly to the same Table, and shewes him *Hyanisbe's* Letter; which as he was reading, *Meleander* falls upon his neck; and then the young Prince, prostrate at his feet, with change of countenance, and a farre other manner of duty, then such as he had before used towards him, much distracted their thoughts that stood about him. But this sight did most of all trouble *Poliarchus* : Should he see his Corrivall taken to imbraces, and entertayned with all the shew of most heartie affection, while he in the meane time stood neglected by *Meleander*, and left alone to hold discourse with *Eurymedes*? For, he, out of good manners, came close to him, while *Meleander* was in talke with *Archombrotus*, that that King might not be unmannerly left alone in the midst of the roome. As he was swelling with rage for this indignity offered him, there hapned a new cause of fiercer indignation : for, *Argenis* being told, her Father called for her, enters the roome : and when the King at her coming whispered something in her eare, that none else could heare, and *Archombrotus* offered her a kisse, she most affectionately with both her hands claspes him about the necke. Then both of them shed teares, which by their other lookes and gestures seemed to proceed from their fulnesse of joy; and she gave her hand to *Archombro-*

tus

tus at his requeſt, in pledge of a moſt indiſſoluble love.

Now had fury overcome *Poliarchus* his patience, and he was in minde to diſturbe this new joy of theirs, that ſo much vexed him.   Not knowing whom he ſhould moſt curſe, *Hyanisbe*, *Meleander*, or *Archombrotus*, he was much more incenſed againſt *Argenis*, on whom he reſolved to be revenged, at leaſtwiſe by killing himſelfe : and, as thought, eſpecially angry thought, is ever ſwifter then ſpeech, he had in a ſhort time many and cruell cogitations : Hath *Hyanisbe* then, after her preſervation by the wounds of me and my ſubjects, thus rewarded me ? I, unprovident man, expoſed my ſelfe to her poyſons, and accepted of her Phyſicians in my ſickneſſe : but ſhe would not have me dye, till I firſt found my ſelfe ſlighted and ſcorned to my face, and ſee *Argenis* not onely given away from me, but ſo farre bewitched, as to hang upon her Sonnes necke. Haſt thou ſent me, thou Witch, to ſo bitter an end ? Are theſe your Letters, theſe your promiſes, theſe your vowes made in the hearing of your houſhold gods ? Oh foole that I was, to hope for truth in *Africa* ! But you ſhall not ſcape without revenge for your treachery. I will have warre with thee, I will (by *Hercules*) have warre to the utter ruine of thy whole Nation.   Why doe I thus ſtand muſing, like a foole ? and, as if I had a minde to live, cheriſh my ſelfe with hope of future comforts ? Seeſt thou not ſome here before thee, who, it is fit, ſhould dye, and thy ſelfe with them ? I will goe and take that hang-mans breathe from him, that having obtayned the Crowne of *Sardinia* by my conqueſt, makes now no queſtion but to fore-ſtall mee in my marriage ; and I will make the ſhameleſſe *Argenis* looke redde at leaſt, and bluſh with his blond : Then will I cut in pieces this miſchievous old man, this Goblin, this Ghoſt, before any can come to his reſcue : and for *Argenis* her ſelfe ; *Argenis*, I ſay——. (Here, wretched man, hee ſtopped in his cruell reſolution.) But what will it avayle

meeto let a poore Maid bloud? Shee will fitlier dye with
the memory of her owne falshood, and my wound. I
will rip up mine owne heart, and when the bloud shall
gush out, caft my felfe upon her, like a Fury, to affright
her: for, if I were not refolved fo to dye, I could raife my
owne Souldiers; I could with my owne fafety, plucke
downe thefe buildings upon my enemies heads. But I will
not live, for feare to bee reconciled to *Argenis.*

Hee had no leifure to caft in his minde thofe and fuch
like defperate conceits, while their firft mutuall loving
entertainment made *Meleander, Archombrotus,* and *Argenis,*
forget all other bufineffe: and being thus head-ftrong and
refolute in his purpofe, had his hand upon his Swords
hilt, when the gods would not fuffer fo good a man to be
guilty of fo foule a crime: Even at that very inftant, *Mele-*
ander, nothing knowing of all this rage of his, and comming to him; Pardon us, faid hee, deare Gueft, for that
wee have beene ftayed from giving you fit entertainment,
by an unexpected gladneffe, which peradventure will be no
leffe pleafing to you, then even now you perceived it to be
to me and *Argenis.* Come, deareft of mortall men, partner of
our happineffe, and fee what this day hath deferved of you.

Poliarchus wholly altered with this fpeech, and in this
change of affections doubtfull what to expect or thinke,
refufed not to goe with *Meleander.* But when they came
clofe to *Archombrotus* and *Argenis;* then *Meleander,* not
now with fo low a voyce, but that the Souldiers by,
might heare, Oh, fruitfull day, quoth hee, oh day pro-
pitious to thefe yeeres of mine, who heretofore content
to folace my felfe with one onely Daughter, am now blef-
fed with two, two fuch children! Let not the gods envy
mee. What mortall is now happier then my felfe am? or,
who fhould make more account of the poore remainder of
life, that is left him? Did then the Fates, through fo many
croffes, and threatning dangers prepare mee thefe aydes
and

and ornaments of my Kingdome? Cease, dearest Guest, greatest of Kings, and (which is more then all) *Poliarchus*, to be angry with *Archombrotus*. It is long since I perceived you were at difference. Both of you loved *Argenis*, and both of you shall enjoy her: for, hee whom I have begotten, shall love her as a Sister: and to you, if you bee not otherwise disposed, I give her for your wife: for, though by finding a Brother, shee hath lost the Inheritance of *Sicily*; yet neverthelesse, if I bee not deceived in you, you will love her, and she shall be a Queene: for *Sardinia*, and whatsoever belonged to *Radirobanes* (which indeed is your gift to *Archombrotus*) shall be her Dower. Thus hath my Son agreed with me: and now, *Archombrotus*, do you first renounce all hatred, and give your Sister to King *Poliarchus*.

Who would have thought so much? *Archombrotus* labouring the Match, and offering his Sisters hand, invites *Poliarchus* to the marriag of *Argenis* while he in this chang of fortune could hardly beleeve his own happinesse. And *Argenis* blushed; she, that while the warres, and her Father, crossed her; she, that not long was so bold, so almost rebellious against her Father, & would follow *Poliarchus* wheresoever he listed; now remembred she was a Virgin. *Poliarchus* all at once gives his hand to *Argenis*, thanks *Meleander*; and withall wonders, by what meanes *Archombrotus* was so suddenly become Brother to *Argenis*. Then, as is usuall in great and sudden chances, they all talked confusedly; all without order, all together. The young Princes renewed their old friendship, which they had begun at *Timoclea's* house. The old King, and the young Lady had got fresh spirit: and the chearefulnesse of the young Kings spred it selfe amongst all the beholders. The Noblemen stood mute for a time, and afterwards filled the whole Court with variety of discourse. And many preased in, to heare the newes. Neither was *Meleander* displeased with this concourse of people: for, it concerned him to have so

Aaa2   great

great and publique businesse generally knowne. An d
therefore with a cleare voyce, as if the old mans joy had
given him strength, My good subjects and Guests, said h e,
whom this day hath drawne into a most sacred unity and
friendship ; goe all, gratulate your Kings, and spend the
rest of the Day in holy exercise. I would have you all to
morrow to come to the Court Gate. There shall both
the people and the Souldiers be assembled, that none may
be ignorant of the blessings of the gods, which, I thinke,
they have more abundantly bestowed upon mee, then
upon any other : Yet I thinke It fit you should in few
words understand the cause of my so exceeding gladnesse.
I have found out, that *Archombrotus* is my owne sonne :
my Wife was delivered of him, unknowne to me : and
my Daughter shall bee married to King *Poliarchus.* Goe
merrily home, and make this happy day, if you please,
the Vigill to the morrowes joy. I, in the meane time,
with my Sonne-in-law, and Sonne, will dispose of our
affaires, as we shall thinke fit.

CHAP. XIX.

Great joy amongst the Sicilians, French *and* Africanes. Meleander *calleth together the people, and causeth the Letter of*
Hyanisbe *to bee read in publique.*

AFter the dismission of the Nobles, hee tooke
Poliarchus into his privat Lodging, intending
to solace himselfe that night with the sweet
society of his dearest friends. What wishes
had each of them then? What thoughts? The
most chast *Argenis* enjoyed the fruit of her constancy, and
had wonne so much by her many griefes, that none could
seeme worthier of her great fortune, then her selfe. *Poliar-*
chus

chus, now forgetting all emulation and grudge, tooke pleasure, when his Father-in-law jested upon him, for the kisses that *Argenis* had in sisterly affection given to *Archombrotus*. Then *Meleander* laughed at them both; sometimes calling *Archombrotus* his Sonne-in-law; and sometimes calling *Poliarchus*, *Theocrine*. And *Archombrotus* asked *Argenis*, what shee was most glad of, upon her first true knowledge of him; whether it were, that shee had him her brother, or should not have him for her Husband? Amongst these jests, their mirth hardly gave them leisure for businesses. *Aneroestus* himselfe laid aside his austerity, and presumed to bee merry; and though in course attyre, yet he was used royally, as a King, both by *Meleander* and *Argenis*. There were but few of their most pryvate friends admitted to this chearefull recreation. And yet *Aneroestus*, *Iburranes*, and *Dunalbius* supped with the Kings: and *Gelanorus*, *Arsidas* and *Gobrias* were present, with *Micipsa* the *Mauritanian*, and *Cleobulus* and *Eurymedes*. *Nicopompus* was twice sent for by the King, but stayed somewhat too long: for hee had retyred himselfe to make the *Epithalamion*. *Timoclea* only, of all the Ladies, attended on *Argenis*. These were all that waited upon the King at this Supper. All their chiefe discourse was of *Poliarchus*; how heartily he had loved; how forgetting his owne estate, hee had thrust himselfe into dangers, unknowne, carelesse of himselfe; and farre from safety; either from Fortune, or his enemies hatred. From whence should this ardour arise? or what ground had hee to build so constant a love upon? Then did hee relate to those willing hearers, how hee had heard a large report of the beauty and vertue of *Argenis*, in *France*; hence grew an earnest desires in his youthfull heart; which the admiration of her rare perfections, or (to speake more truely) the Fates augmented; and when hee knew that the *Sicilian* Lawes forbad any marriage with the *French*, that barre did

did so much the more enflame him: and thereupon preten-
ding a devotion to the gods of forreine Nations, and under colour to visit their Temples, he came privately with
Gelanorus into *Sicily*, that hee might bee an eyewitnesse,
whether the beauty of *Argenis* were answerable to the report that went of her, and worthy of the warre he intended to make against those Lawes of *Sicily*; if he could win
her affection, as hee hoped in time to doe, and nothing
but those Lawes hindered his happinesse. But when hee
was come into *Sicily*, he could not so much as have a sight
of the Lady, who being shut up in a strong Castle, it was
not lawfull for any man to see her. Then hee resolved to
put himselfe upon that happy hazard, to come in a Vir-
gins habit, to beguile *Selenissa*, and to bee called *Theo-*
crine. *Meleander* helped him out with the rest of the story,
often remembring between mirth and admiration, how
in all poynts like a Maid hee came, with what a mournfull
tale hee had moved him to compassion, and so made himselfe way to *Argenis*; and after, with what exceeding
courage and strength hee had quelled the Villaines, that
were entred the Castle; and of *Theocrine*, became *Pal-*
las.

Then they turned their discourse from *Poliarchus* to *Ar-*
chombrotus, and wondred at many passages concerning
him. Was hee then the true Prince of *Sicily*, and had so
loved *Meleander*, not knowing whom he honoured? how
long *Hyanisbe* had concealed this land in how seasonable a
time discovered it! How the gods had brought all this to
passe, not much unlike the pleasure of a devised Fable in
a Comedy! Then *Meleander* discoursed his marriage in
Africa, and, as farre as the present mirth gave leave, be-
wayled his dead wife; and so by often telling all this
story, with his severall adventures, hee seemed to di-
gest the speech hee was the next day to make in publique.

                                                    The

The night was farre spent, when they rose from Supper. When it was neere Sunne-rising, all that were in *Palermo* flocked with Garlands of greene boughs on their heades, to the Court. The Court-yards were not able to containe the multitude. Some got up upon the walls and some filled the Scaffolds that were set up on purpose. Others brought Ladders, many of which breaking with their too heavy burden, fell upon those that were under them. At the Palace Gate was a little Scaffold built, almost to a mans height. There were the Chayres of State set for the Kings, two of equall height; where *Poliarchus* and *Meleander* sate; and two somewhat lower towards the side of the Scaffold for *Archombrotus* and *Argenis*.

When the Princes were seated, and the Herald had proclaimed silence, *Meleander*, after a little pauze, thus began: if I were to acquaint you (my good Guests and Subjects,) with any disastrous businesse, I had need to use Art and Eloquence to mitigate the danger, and cheare up your hearts. But, as it is, what need I with vaine flourishes of speech to set forth the benefit of the gods, which they have so bountifully bestowed upon us? I bring you joyfull tydings, of peace and amity with our confederate Kings and Nations; and terrour, warre, and desolation to our Enemies. Nor doe I thinke, but you know, what I am about to speake. Some god, no doubt, and Fame her selfe, if Shee hath any Deity, hath given you notice, that this day is to bee the day of my daughters marriage with King *Poliarchus*; and, as it were, the new birth-day of my Sonne; (and with that he turned his looke towards *Archombrotus*, that was rising to him) who, why he hath continued so long unknowne to mee, and how I have now found him to be my sonne; it is very fit (my loving Subjects) you all should know. Here, Herald, take the Queene of *Mauritania's* Letter, and reade it openly, as loud as thy voyce will serve thee.

Then

Then the Herald read the Letter, to this purpose:

Queene *Hyanisbe* to King *Meleander*, health.

I Know not, whether to ascribe it to your vertue, or your fault, that I have not thought good till this day, to make you a sharer in that exceeding joy, which now, to your wonder, I shall impart unto you: for, I hold it your fault, that you would neither acquaint mee with your marriage with my sister Anna; nor, after her death, ever make inquiry, whether you had any issue by her: yet I did so much honour your vertue, that I would not deliver you your owne Son, till I had first made triall, whether he would grow worthy of so great a Father: But now finding his worth answerable to his birth, I thought fit to discover what I kept so long concealed. When you at your departure towards Sicily, left my Sister Anna here, whom you had not long before secretly married, and the time was expired, wherein shee had by many devices sought to cover her great belly, at last shee fell exceeding sicke: We, mistaking her disease, gave her unprofitable physicke: But shee finding her end to draw on, thus spake to mee in private: Pardon mee, deare Sister, since I have not otherwise offended, but in my silence: I am Wife to Meleander King of Sicily: I am now upon the poynt of my delivery; and my paines are such, as I feare mee, I cannot escape death: If my Childe live, deare Sister, I leave it to your choyce, whether you will keepe it, or send it to the Father: yet would I have this kept secret, that the people may not know I was a Mother, before I was a Wife. But we had severall reasons to keepe our marriage private; both, because wee stood in feare, that Cirthus the Numidian, my unwelcome Suiter, would use some violence: and for that Meleander desired to bee married in Royall State, and to that end hasted home; add lastly, in respect of my shamefastnesse, which I am afraid (miserable woman!) I doe now violate, even with the telling you this Story. See (Sister) heere on my Pillow lye the conditions of our Marriage under Meleanders owne hand, whereto for confirmation I also put mine. (And withall she delivered me the writing. But in this Boxe are certaine private notes of our secret

contract

contract; as Letters, Rings, and a Bracelet made of both our
haire. When you shall shew him these, hee will know, I have
imparted unto you the truth of all passages betweene us. At these
words, her speech fayled her, I comforted her, after a little re-
covery of strength, calling some of her most trusty women to her,
and wee all tooke care for things needfull for her. But her throwes
exceeded all our helpe: yet was shee delivered of a Sonne, which wee
held to her, while shee was yet living: and then I asked of her, if
shee could endure to write some few words. I know not what god put-
ing mee in minde to have her doe that, which is now so availeable to
our present businesse. She did so at my request, and writ, that shee
was then dying, and left your Sonne to my education. You will
know her hand (excellent King) though through weakenesse and
trembling shee could not well guide her Pen, nor draw her Letters
right. Not long after, shee dyed in my armes. There were onely
foure women with me. I delivered the Infant to one Sophoneme, one whom I especially trusted, with charge to take care of him,
and found him out a Nurse, that did not know whose Childe shee was
to keepe. And fearing lest any of these foure should prove blabs,
I afterwards deceived them also, by the helpe of the same Sophoneme, making them beleeve the Boy was dead. About the same
time my Brother Iuba dyed, and left me his Kingdome: and my
Husband Syphax, as if the Fates had conspired against us, ended
his life. Beeing thus full of griefe, yet I neither forgot you, Meleander, nor my Sister, I counterfeited my selfe with child, and
with the same Sophoneme's helpe gave out, that I was delivered of a Sonne, after my husbands death. But I could not then
shew your Sonne, as my owne: for the child was too big to be new-
borne. But Sophoneme supplyed his roome with another new-
borne babe, which afterwards shee, by my appointment, put to nurse.
I, making shew to feare, the Child might bee bewitched, gave
charge, that none but the Nurses and Sophoneme alone, should
be suffered to see my Sonne. And then after two yeeres, it was easie
to shew your Hyempsal (for so his dying mother named him, after

kis

his Grandfathers name) for my owne Sonne. And ever since, I
have kept my selfe a widdow for his sake, and meane to leave him
my Kingdome. None of our neighbour Kings could with any suite
draw me to marriage. When he was three and twenty yeeres old, I
made report to him of your vertues, and advised him to travell into Sicily; to see the manner of your government, and learne to
rule by your example. And that he might compasse this with more
ease, if hee would goe as a private man, and not bee knowne that I
was his Mother; lest your favour, and the flattery of others, might
carry him quite away from that fresh and reall vertue, which being
often denyed to Princes, ennobles the actions and estates of meaner
men. He, in obedience to my command, went thither : and it is
wonderfull that hee should winne so much upon your affection, that
you, being so great a King, should offer to bestow on him your Daughter, borne of your last wife, having (as you thought) no more children. When he had written this newes to me, though I was glad of
his vertue and your nature, which drew you to love your yet unknowne Sonne; yet I trembled with the feare of the mention of such
an incestuous marriage, lest the Brother should marry his owne
Sister. And I was frighted also with other dangers, for Radirobanes was comming to the spoyle of Africa with his Army. I
therefore wrote to our Hyempsal, whom you call Archombrotus, to put off the marriage, which I heare, is concluded betweene
you; and to request him to make all speede with his Navy to my
succour. But his helpe had come too late, neither had hee found
whom he should have relieved, if the storme had not cast King Poliarchus with his French Forces upon our Coast. By his valour are
the spoyles of Radirobanes now in our Temple of Mars. But we
were like to have had more fatall differences in peace, than in
warre; through the bitter emulation of Poliarchus and Archombrotus. Your Argenis was the cause of their hatred, whose
marriage both of them seeke, beyond the common desire of men. I
finding your Sonnes fury and mistaking, prevailed with them,
both to bridle their rage, and abstaine from fight, till they had delivered

*livered you this Letter, and instantly each of them should be master
of his wishes : which will so come to passe, if you bee pleased to acknowledge your Sonne, and give your Daughter to wife to King
Poliarchus; than whom, no man this day breathing, commeth neerer
to the gods in noble atchievements, and heroicall vertues. I give
you full power to make her a Dower either out of your estate or
mine : Sicily, Mauritania, and the late conquered Sardinia,
will bee enough both for your Sonne to raigne in plenty, and to bestow your daughter according to her birth and estate. I send you in
this Cabinet, whatsoever secret my Sister left me on her death-bed;
and amongst the rest, her last letter, wherein shee gives you to understand, that shee had a sonne of yours come into the world, when
she left it. All which were once lately lost : for (O mischiefe!) the
Pirates had robbed mee of the Cabinet. But King Poliarchus
slew the Theeves, and brought it me backe untouched. So you are
in part indebted to him for your Sonne; and I for my Kingdome,
whereto I have long agoe designed your Hyempsal for my successor.
No reward, but Argenis, can be sufficient for these his many merits. Farewell, and cheere up your old age with these blessings bestowed upon you by the gods.*

The hoarse Herald could scarcely reade over this long
Letter. After the reading of it, followed a confused
noyse among the people. Many had heard it; and they
which stood further off, troubled those that understood
it, with multiplicity of questions. The Letter also seemed
very darke to many of them; which *Meleander* thinking
before-hand it would so fall out, began to explane the
Letter with another speech of his owne. Hee rehearsed
the whole story of his youth; how at his Fathers command, hee had heretofore married the Daughter of the
Prince of the *Brutians*, who continuing his wife sixe yeeres
without issue, dyed of a hurt shee tooke by a fall from her
horse, as she was hunting, against a stubbe of a tree. He was
then thirty five yeeres old, his Father still living. At the
same

fame time raigned in *Mauritania*, *Iuba*, a Confederate with
Sicily, to whom hee travelled with a fmall traine, to drive
away the griefe he had for the death of his wife.   Then
he told them, how King *Iuba* had two Sifters; the elder of
them, *Hyanisbe*, married to *Syphax*, a man there of great
power and eftate : the younger called *Anna*, who had a
Suiter, one *Cirtbus*, a Numidian; a Prince of fo great power,
that *Iuba*, though hee liked him not, feared to offend him.
How hee himfelfe in the meane time fell in love with the
Lady *Anna*, who hating the Numidian, caft her affection
upon him.   So they were married privately; and he, by
her advice, returned home, to gather forces out of *Sicily*,
to oppofe the Numidian, if hee fhould offer any open violence; and there was ftayed by his Father Funerall, that he
could not returne, at the time he promifed, into *Africa*.
In this *interim* hee had newes brought him of the death of
the Lady *Anna*; and fo, no more minding *Mauritania*, he
afterwards married a Sicilian Lady, his Uncles Daughter,
by whom hee had *Argenis*.   The reft you have, my good
Subjects, out of Queene *Hyanisbe's* letter; how fhe fucceeded her brother *Iuba* in the Kingdome, and how the Lady
Anna was delivered of this my Sonne.   Shee hath heere
fent me many infallible tokens of the truth, in a Cabinet
locked and fealed up; all which I well know, by the remembrance of fore-paffed accidents.

CHAP. XX.

CHAP. XX.

Poliarchus *married to* Argenis. Nicopompus *his Epithala-mium.* Archombrotus *espoused to* Poliarchus *his absent Sister.* Aneroestus *his prediction of happinesse to them all.*

Hen looking upon *Poliarchus;* By what name, said hee, shall I call you, most mighty King, whose gift it is, that wee live and raigne? You freed both me and *Argenis* from slavery, when the villaines sent by *Lycogenes,* broke into her lodgings. You, in the front of my Army, led my Souldiers to victory; and you alone vanquished my enemies. Afterwards, you left *Sicily,* to my hurt, and, how-ever you would excuse it, to my shame. Neither could our injuries overcome your goodnesse. You were wronged, and yet still loved *Argenis.* What shall I say, how by the conduct of the gods you found these tokens, whereby I have come to the knowledge of my *Sonne,* and hee of his father, amongst the Pirates, and by your valour redeemed them? And in *Africa,* what a hard and glorious worke to keepe *Radirobanes* from Conquest, the losse of your bloud, which still appeareth by the palenesse of your face, well declares. Would you could love a name, that might shew mee to bee inferiour to you. But you had rather have mee called your Father-in-law. Oh happy *Argenis,* in so great a match! You have by your vertue shewed us the folly of that cowardly policy of our Ancestors, who did so much feare the greatnesse of the French, that they straitly forbade our *Sicilian* Princes to marry with yours, as if so great and powerfull alliance were to be held as a servitude. You
have

have deserved, that we should all with one consent abrogate this Law, but the gods have so dealt with us, as wee have no need to breake this Ordinance : For, they have restored me my Sonne, to succeed me in *Sicily*, and my *Argenis* shall not be of meaner estate; for she shall have *Sardinia* and *Liguria*, and unite them to your *France*, without breach of our Lawes. Heere *Archombrotus*, as it was agreed, asked leave of his Father to speake; and presently begun to *Poliarchus* in this manner : The possession of *Sardinia*, which I enjoy, what is it else, but the fruit of your victory ? You conquered it in *Africa*; I came onely to the Triumph. You therefore, dearest Sister; you, for loving of whom, *Poliarchus* himselfe doth now pardon me, receive heere this Crowne, and in liew of *Sicily*, whereto my birthright hath intitled me; be you Queene of all the dominions which were under *Radirobanes*. You shall bring that to your Husband, which he, in right of his victory, might have taken as his owne. And withall, he puts the Crowne upon his Sisters head; *Meleander* weeping for joy, and the people applauding it with so many and lowd acclamations, that for a long time their eares lost their office. *Poliarchus*, as he was exceedingly eloquent, extenuated so the memory of his merits, as indeed he did cunningly set them forth to the most; with such reverence to *Meleander*, and faire demeanour to *Archombrotus*, *Argenis*, and the people, that it was questionable, whether hee were the braver Warriour or Courtier.

And now, as they were all setting forward to the Temple, *Nicopompus* his Sonne, that was little above tenne yeeres old, was brought by his Father to *Argenis*, and smiling, delivered her an *Epithalamion*, made by his Father, and in a bold and jesting manner, affirmed himselfe to bee the Author of it. And when *Meleander* called him to him, and willed him to give him and *Poliarchus* copies, of it; the Boy did so, having some ready written

in

in his hand.   They continuing to question him, whose
worke the Verses were, forced him often to smile at the
telling of his lye. There were but a few lines as to Princes
that were now busied: and so they found the more readers

> To grace this Marriage from the starry Skie,
> Phœbus descends; you gods we can descrie,
> We, that are Poets. Lo, from th' opened Skie,
> The gods long traine descends to Sicily.
> Whilst Hymen lights his Torch, whilst heav'ns great Queene
> Adornes the Bridall pompe, and Cupid's seene
> To deale his gentle wounds, and misses not;
> Behold, faire Phœbus his crown'd Harp had got,
> To which his rosie lips gan tune this note:
>   Ioyne in a lasting league your loving hands,
> Which Time shall not dissolve, nor Fates withstand;
> Ioyne, Princes; On you smile these golden dayes;
> Hymen is here; Oh, crowne your Posts with Bayes,
> And let the five-fold bridall Tapers shine,
> Whilst the French gods with the Sicilian joyne.
> Blest Father-in-law! blest paire! blest Progenie!
>   Behold the Virgins face, long promis'd thee;
> Such are Minerva's cheekes; such are the faire
> Saturnia's eyes; such Cytherea's haire;
> Like Cynthia, when her hunting Robes she leaves;
> And her the Skie in brightest lookes receives,
> Is thy faire Bride. The gods benignity,
> Great King, behold; but with a neerer eye,
> Survey her beauteous mind: Thou'lt thinke her heart
> Not mortall; and that thou in heaven art.
>   As much, thy lookes, and golden lockes to see,
> Thy chaste flame-sparkling eyes, rejoyces thee.
> Sometimes her loving heart fancies thee, so,
> As thou to warre in dreadfull Armes dost goe;
> Sometimes thy lookes, when forth at thy returne

Thy Subjects flocke; when in like triumph borne,
Her selfe shall Gallia's longing Cities view,
Sometimes shee thinkes shee dreames; Too good for true
Is what shee sees, and fading when shee wakes.
    Ah, feare not, Princely Maid; No slumber makes
This joy, nor are thy longing thoughts deluded,
'Tis true; the gods with mee have all concluded.
Thus with one heart and voyce they all command;
Ioyne in a lasting league your loving hands;
Oh, joyne your hands, thou, of all Maids most bright,
Thou, amongst men, such, as in cleerest night,
Bright Lucifer *does other Starres excell.*
But come thou, sacred Peace, at length, and dwell
With these deserving brests; Enough have they
Endur'd of danger, and enough delay.
Now make these Princes in each other blest,
And of their long-desired jeyes possest.
Not great Alcides *entred heaven, before*
That he the sweat of his twelue labours wore.
    Your loving hands conjoyne for aye in one;
Oh, joyne your hands. All Clouds and stormes are gone.
A gentler Ayre now shines; no day shall lowre,
And all the gods on you their gifts shall powre.
Though in sad stormes great Heroes *fortunes ever*
Begin; yet Vertue suffers shipwracke never.

The Sacrifices were prepared at the Temple of *Iuno Lucina*; and the *Augures*, and the High-priests, in order ready to beginne their devotions for the prosperous successe of the marriage. The people sung Hymnes to *Hymen*, and *Pæans* to *Apollo*. But because *Argenis* had not a Mother, to carry the Torch before her at her marriage; that Honour, upon the commendation of *Poliarchus* and *Archombrotus*, was conferred upon *Timoclea* : They called upon the gods of Marriage, and chiefly on the guardians of the fires
that

that were borne before *Argenis*, who was covered with
a veyle; when now the Sacrifices being ready to be slaine,
Poliarchus, more majestically than before, by reason of
this dayes joy, commands the Sacrificers to stay their
hands, and thus speakes to *Archombrotus*: If you will beleeve me, Brother; it grieves mee, that now when I am
married, you should bee to seeke a wife. I have a Sister,
whose beauty and naturall endowments would much
commend one of meaner estate; about twenty yeeres of
age. To make our friendship the stronger, I will, if you
please, give her to you in marriage. And because, by the
Law of our Countrey, no part of the Kingdome can de-
scend upon a Daughter, her Dower shall bee six hundred
Talents in present money. *Meleander* was present at this
proposition, who, when *Archombrotus* made a little pawse,
not so much staying to give his consent, (for this alliance
pleased him well) but as leaving this choyse of his wife to
his Father, asked him, If hee would accept the Lady upon these conditions. And *Poliarchus* also wished *Argenis*,
though shee then at those holy Rites kept silence, to move
her brother to this marriage. He, with open and cheere-
full countenance, answered, that hee gladly accepted this
offer, and embracing *Poliarchus*; You have, said hee, most
puissant King, prevented my wishes. What god hath re-
vealed to you the secrets of my heart? let mee then also be
espowsed to the absent Lady; even with these Rites. You,
my dearest Brother, shall engage your faith for us both.
The Priests were willed to double the Ceremonies; which
they did, making a great coyle about the Temple with
their speed and diligence. And when the newes was brui-
ted among the people, the ayre being fill'd with the fresh
shouts and acclamations of the applauding Multitude;
some few Birds that flew over them, losing the helpe of
their wings, fell downe dead amongst them. All men
rejoyced: all men runne up and downe, as if their joy had

loſt them their wits: and in this confuſed multitude, their
exceſſe of mirth made them forget all difference of perſons.

In the meane time they offered, what they had cut out
of the inwards of the Sacrifices, to the gods: and when the
Augures told them, all happineſſe was portended by the
Oblations, one of which had a liver made like a garland;
the Incenſe being kindled, the Princes that were to bee
married, approched to the Altar. After the Rites ended,
the whole Trayne was returning to the Court, when in
the Porch of the Temple, *Aneroſtus* meetes them at their
comming forth, with a pale countenance, full of Pro-
phetique fury: for the gods had poſſeſſed his deſerving
breſt. So, ſhaking his reverend head with a divine rage;
Haile, ſaid he, Oh Kings: Oh the ſpeciall care of the gods;
heretofore uſed to croſſes and afflictions, but now comming to find by experience, that nothing brings more
perfect felicity, then vertue. Ah, happieſt old man! doe
not upbraid the gods, *Meleander*, for ſpending of your
time in warre, and the rebellion of your Subjects: You
ſhall yet enjoy many yeeres of a ſtrong and healthfull life,
and neither feare forraign nor domeſticke violence. You
ſhall ſometimes viſite *Hyanisbe* in *Africa*, and ſometimes
entertaine her in *Sicily*. All faction and Treaſon ſhall
bee farre from your Raigne. Your age, and *Archombrotus* his youth, ſhall ſtrike reverence and terrour into all
Nations. You, happy Father, ſhall ſee him returning
with victory and triumph from your neighbouring *Breti-
ans*, *Lucanes*, and *Epeireians*: and his children ſhall grow
to yeeres in your imbraces, and leave a long ſucceſſion
of Princes to the Crowne of *Sicily*. Neither is your Daughter dearer unto you, that now muſt depart for *France*, then
your Daughter-in-law ſhall bee, that is to come from
thence. But you; Jewels of this age; you, *Poliarchus*
and *Argenis*; doe not thinke at this time to heare of thoſe
reward

rewards, that are most certainely laid up in store for your conftancy and vertue. Many things I know not: many things I muft not fpeake. The Fates themfelves keepe fome part of the happineffe to which you are borne, concealed even from the gods, left they fhould envy you. Yet take thus much from mee: That love, which hath this day joyned you together, fhall hold inviolate to the end. No difference, no loathing, no jealoufie fhall leffen it. The *Rhine* on the one fide, and the Ocean on the other, fhall behold you Conquerours. The Statues of *Timandra* fporting among her Nephewes, fhall be miftaken, by the happy errour of our Pofterity, for *Cybele*, the Mother of the gods. The neighbour-Nations fhall admire your glory and power; and not refufe, to bee conquered, to bee governed by you. Wherefoever you goe, Safety her felfe fhall attend you: whatfoever you defire, the gods fhall prevent your wifhes. And, that your felicity leave you not even in death, one night fhall (after a long and happy age) cloze up both your eyes together, and fend you to increafe the number of the Starres. Nor doubt yee of your fame: That fhall bee made eternall by the *Genius* of your Hiftory, which hereafter fhall bee fpred abroad among all Nations; and no force, no time bee able to extinguifh it.

FJ NJS.

*For Product Safety Concerns and Information please contact
our EU representative GPSR@taylorandfrancis.com Taylor & Francis
Verlag GmbH, Kaufingerstraße 24, 80331 München, Germany*

T - #0057 - 270225 - C0 - 246/189/9 [11] - CB - 9780754604419 - Gloss Lamination